Wisdom With
Understanding
is Better
Than Rubies

Lurine Karon Greenberg
Fine Arts Collection

African Americans and the Oscar

Seven Decades of Struggle and Achievement

By Edward Mapp

The Scarecrow Press, Inc.
Lanham, Maryland, and Oxford
2003

SCARECROW PRESS, INC.

Published in the United States of America
by Scarecrow Press, Inc.
A Member of the Rowman & Littlefield Publishing Group
4501 Forbes Boulevard, Suite 200
Lanham, Maryland 20706
www.scarecrowpress.com

PO Box 317
Oxford
OX2 9RU, UK

British Cataloging in Publication Information Available

Library of Congress Cataloging-in-Publication Data

Mapp, Edward.
    African Americans and the Oscar : seven decades of struggle and
achievement / Edward Mapp.
        p. cm.
    Includes bibliographical references and index.
    ISBN 0-8108-4788-4 (alk. paper)
    1. African Americans in motion pictures. 2. African American
motion picture actors and actresses—United States—Bibliography.
3. Academy Awards (Motion pictures) I. Title.
PN1995.9.N4M29 2003
791.43'028'092273—dc21   2003007563

To Oscar Devereaux Micheaux (1884–1951),
African American filmmaker.

Courtesy of the author

Contents

Contents

Introduction

The Oscar[1] is the most sought after prize in the film industry. To understand what the hullabaloo is about, one must appreciate the symbolism and value of the Oscar trophy. Academy Award winner Joan Crawford once said, "I don't think the public knows what Oscar means to us. It is one of the most emotional things that can happen to a human being." The results of a research study published in the Annals of Internal Medicine (2001) suggest that Oscar winners live longer than their non–Academy Award winning counterparts. Longevity aside, filmmakers still view the winning of an Oscar as the acme of their careers. The Oscar is a metaphor for success. On a purely practical basis, it proves useful in the promotion of films.

The first Oscars were presented for the 1927–1928 years. The year of citation is the year of the honored work: the actual Oscar ceremony occurs early the following year. Emil Jannings won the first best actor award for *The Last Command* and *The Way of All Flesh*, while Janet Gaynor won the first best actress award for *Seventh Heaven*, *Street Angel*, and *Sunrise*.

Cedric Gibbons, MGM art director, created the design of "Oscar" by responding to a request for a symbol that would depict continuing progress in the industry and that was both militant and dynamic. Gibbons came up with the figure of a man with a crusader's sword, standing on a reel of film.

Bette Davis, two time winner, claims she named the trophy because it reminded her of the backside of her then husband Harmon "Oscar" Nelson. Academy librarian and executive secretary Margaret Herrick stakes her claim for its name, saying the statuette resembled her uncle "Oscar" Pierce. Columnist Sidney Skolsky swears he was the first to print the name "Oscar" in his column.

To understand why there have been so few African Americans honored, one must be aware of the complex procedures and the elaborate process in place. The Academy of Motion Picture Arts and Sciences (AMPAS) is small compared to the other screen organizations, which in part accounts for charges of elitism. The Academy's prestige stems somewhat from its membership eligibility requirements—invitation of two members or being nominated for an award. Membership is lifelong. African Americans represent less than 5 percent of the membership, which consequently impacts on the number of black nominees. Critics of the Academy's system for selecting award recipients must be reminded that it is not a small group of white males in a Wilshire Boulevard suite making the choices. There is no such thing as a monolithic Academy that either grants or denies nominations and awards. The Academy is only as impartial as the sum of its constituent parts.

All eligible members vote on nominations for best picture. Films must have been screened for at least one week in theaters in New York or Los Angeles before December 31 to be eligible for Academy Award consideration. Nominations in the acting categories are voted on only by the membership of that branch, that is, acting. The membership of the Academy's Actors Branch is approximately one-fourth of the Academy's voting membership. When it comes to the acting categories, the Academy tends to be permissive. Any performance by an actor or actress in any role is eligible in either the leading role or supporting category. The selection of an actor as a lead or in support has become increasingly unpredictable. The dividing line between a leading role and supporting role nomination is arbitrary because it is often the combined judgment call of the studio, the filmmaker, and to a lesser extent the performer in question. Publicity campaigns and critically favorable notices can tilt the balance.

Most importantly, the results of all Oscar voting are known only to the accounting firm of PricewaterhouseCoopers until the sealed envelopes are opened during the ceremony.

Campaigning for an Oscar is prevalent and indigenous to the politics of Hollywood. Videos of films are mailed to Academy members with a "For Your Consideration" note. In an attempt to assure the integrity of the nominating process, the Academy recently issued a strict set of guidelines aimed at dissuading, if not banning, the blatant solicitation of votes.

In 2002, the Academy issued a six-page list of "dos and don'ts." The stiffening of rules bars studios from sending both a video and a DVD to the same eligible voters, because with two submissions, one appears to be a present. Also discouraged are dinners and receptions promoting specific films. In the past, miscellaneous inducements such as books, T-shirts, and other items were included, compromising the original concept of merit in favor of the expenditure of money. The Academy emphasizes, "The more emphatically that all of us can convey to the industry and the wider public excellence in filmmaking is the *only* factor we consider in casting our Academy Award votes, the more reason the world will have to respect our judgment."

Finally, the Academy conducts annual "post-Oscar" review committee meetings to consider complaints, irregularities and suggestions.

The history of the Academy of Motion Picture Arts and Sciences as it relates to African Americans has been occasionally contentious, sometimes conciliatory, and always controversial.

Because Caucasians were routinely cast to play African American characters in films over the years, Academy Award nominations have gone to Flora Robson, who played a mulatto servant in *Saratoga Trunk* (1946), Jeanne Crain, who played a young black woman passing as white in *Pinky* (1949), and Susan Kohner, who played a light-skinned black also passing as white in a remake of *Imitation of Life* (1959). One can only contemplate whether three talented African American actresses might have joined the list of Oscar nominees had they been cast in these roles. There is a prevailing notion that global audiences won't be able to identify with black actors. Evidence seems to support the idea that European and Asian investors prefer leading characters with white, rather than black, faces. It is conceded that, although individual foreigners are probably not racist, the marketplace is. Stereotypes, particularly of African American males, linger. Tom Cruise and Mel Gibson are big sellers abroad, while Denzel Washington and Samuel L. Jackson are not, although both are extremely popular and commercial here in the United States. Regretfully, there appears to be no real effort to market African American actors in the international marketplace. The executives of the film industry make movies they want to see, and since they are predominantly white, it should not be surprising that the roles are for whites. Achieving Academy Award recognition as it relates to African American actors is contingent upon getting Academy-caliber work in order to warrant consideration. In its seventy-five-year history, the Academy's Acting Branch has nominated fifteen African Americans for performances in leading roles and twenty-one for performances in supporting roles. Never before 1972, a banner year for African American nominations, had three African Americans been nominated for leading roles in a single year: Diana Ross in *Lady Sings the Blues*, Cicely Tyson in *Sounder*, and Paul Winfield in *Sounder*. Only seven African Americans have ever won acting Oscars: Hattie McDaniel, Sidney Poitier, Louis Gossett Jr., Denzel Washington, Whoopi Goldberg, Cuba Gooding Jr., and Halle Berry.

A plethora of talent and a dearth of opportunity has prompted various members of the entertainment community to speak out, some seriously, others comedically. A few of these comments follow:

> Journalist, DeWayne Wickham: "Black Oscar nominees are the Halley's comet of the Academy Awards."
>
> Actor-director, Bill Duke: "What people perceive as being good or bad, pretty or ugly, is all in the eye of the beholder, if your eye is not empathetic and you don't understand that an investment in the future of this industry must include people who have different ideas, standards of beauty, ways of looking at film, you're going to keep coming up with the same results."
>
> Actor, Don Cheadle: "We say our experience is different from theirs [whites] but we get mad when we can't get dressed in tuxes and win an Oscar. We need to get past that."
>
> Director-producer, Ousmane Sembene: "The movies were my only escape. I was fascinated by them, but not my father. I remember that on our way back from a day's fishing, he would give me some change to go to the movies. In Ziguinchor, there was a main street with the movie theater on it and I would stop to look at the posters. I do not think that my father ever went to the movies. He would always ask me, 'Why do you like going to see those stupidities of the whites?'"

At various Oscar ceremonies, three different African American comedians have quipped:

Richard Pryor: "I'm here to explain why no black people will ever be nominated."
Eddie Murphy: "The way it's been going it's about every twenty years we get one, we aren't due until 2004."
Chris Rock: "Looking out over the audience, it's like the million white man march."

Clever and incisive remarks are one type of reaction to the problem but responses have also taken the form of action.

Oscar ceremonies have been picketed over the years in the interest of equal opportunity for African Americans. In 1962, a group known as the Hollywood Race Relations Bureau paraded in front of the Santa Monica Civic Auditorium with signs urging "Film Equality for Negroes" and "Negroes Want a Break." Some of the picketers were arrested for disturbing the peace. In 1996, Reverend Jesse Jackson led a boycott of the Oscar ceremony because of the absence of African American nominees. Some picketers carried signs that read, "Who will win best white actor and white actress?" Some observers, although sympathetic to Jackson's goal, accused him of poor timing, given that this particular ceremony was produced by Quincy Jones and hosted by Whoopi Goldberg, both African Americans. One year later, Jackson referred to "an opportunity deficit, not a talent deficit," warning that "Hollywood must do a better job in reflecting the cultural diversity of society. Until then, every Oscar night is a celebration in excluding people of color from fair share, equal opportunity and access, a slap in the face to the American dream of a 'one big tent' society." Jackson categorized the protest as the first step in the fight against institutional racism in the entertainment industry. He described the action as part of a long-term struggle that will be continued. Those who favor militancy point to the 1999 animated film *Tarzan*, which was without a single black character even though it was purportedly set in Africa. Those who view boycotting as an unrealistic protest tool insist that blacks, a large segment of the movie-going audience in spite of their on-screen exclusion, love movies too much to stay away.

African American artists have recently become involved in some alternatives to the Academy Awards. Each year on the eve of the Oscar ceremony, there is a relatively little-known private event staged by members of the African American entertainment community. Informally known as "the Black Oscars," it is not affiliated with the Academy Awards show. Honorees for their work in film during the preceding year receive a special recognition award in the form of an African statuette of the Tree of Life. Proceeds from the dinner benefit a foundation that reaches out to various black charities. Past honorees have included Cuba Gooding Jr., Marianne Jean-Baptiste, Samuel L. Jackson, and Spike Lee.

The National Association of Black Owned Broadcasters (NABOB) presented its Oscar Micheaux Award for Excellence in 1999 to African American film director Carl Franklin.

The annual Independent Spirit Awards has honored various black achievements, such as the film *Down in the Delta* and its leading actress, Alfre Woodard.

Whether African American actors should pursue these avenues of self-validation or continue the struggle for mainstream inclusion is debatable. It would seem feasible for them to do both.

Some years ago, Karl Malden, then president of the Academy, declaimed, "The members of the Academy have done more to combat racial hatred and racial misunderstanding than all the editorial writers in all the newspapers in the world." As well-intentioned as he was, it takes more than a defensive posture to silence the criticism.

It would be worthwhile for the Academy to publicize more widely some of its good faith efforts. One example is the inauguration in 1977 of a Black American Film History Collection, the first of its kind to be developed by a major film-related institution. Hattie McDaniel memorabilia was the initial acquisition, donated by Edgar Goff, McDaniel's grandnephew. Two decades later, the Edward Mapp Collection of more than a thousand black cast film posters was presented to the Academy and cataloged in its Margaret Herrick Library. These historical archives demonstrate the Academy's recognition of the many contributions made by African Americans to American cinema.

To foster a more level playing field for small, independent productions, which are more likely to involve African American artists, the Academy might consider placing a limitation on the amount of money a studio can spend on promoting a film for Oscar consideration. Such a move would be analogous to the government's bid to reform campaign finance funding in the political sector.

The Academy might wish to consider a special award for exceptional achievement by African Americans in film. The award need not be presented annually, but only as warranted in the judgment of the Academy's Board of Governors. The precedent has already been established to honor the contributions of artists like Greta Garbo, Charlie Chaplin, Barbara Stanwyck, Cary Grant, and others who never won competitive Oscars but earned the industry's respect. A special award in the name of Oscar Micheaux, early independent black filmmaker, would not require a stretch from awards currently bestowed in the names of Irving G. Thalberg, Jean Hersholt, and Gordon E. Sawyer.

Certainly the symbolism of a golden triumphant crusader, sword in hand, and its compatibility with the enduring struggle of African Americans in the film industry is hard to ignore.

After years of a Monday-night tradition, the final Oscar ceremony of the twentieth century switched to Sunday night and started a half hour earlier. The annual event, second in viewership only to the Super Bowl, entered a ten-year agreement with the ABC network. The seventy-fourth annual ceremony, in 2002, took place in the Kodak Theater, the Academy's new shared venue on Hollywood Boulevard, just down the street from the Roosevelt Hotel, scene of the first Academy Awards ceremony.

The event became a watershed moment in Oscar history for several reasons. For the first time in thirty years, three black actors (Halle Berry, Denzel Washington, and Will Smith) were nominated for performances in leading roles. For the first time ever, two black males were nominated in the same year as best actor in leading roles. Another highlight of the occasion was the presentation to Sidney Poitier of an honorary Oscar for lifetime career achievement in films. He received two standing ovations. Poitier's 1963 Oscar had been the first awarded to a black man. The ultimate groundbreaking and record setting came with twin victories for Halle Berry as best actress (the first African American actress to receive this honor) and Denzel Washington as best actor (only the second African American to win in this category). Indeed, Oscar history was made in 2002.

The following entries are arranged in chronological order according to the year in which the work was performed (not the year of the ceremony). Each artist is designated as either nominee or winner. A filmography is provided at the end of the volume for each artist included rather than at the end of each entry to avoid unwanted repetition for those artists with more than one entry.

NOTE

1. The terms *Oscar* and *Academy Awards* as used herein mean the annual awards of achievement presented by the Academy of Motion Picture Arts and Sciences.

1939

Hattie McDaniel

b. June 10, 1895, Wichita, Kansas
d. October 26, 1952, San Fernando Valley, California

Winner, Best Supporting Actress, 1939
MAMMY in *Gone with the Wind*

Hattie McDaniel is one of the silver screen's first strong black women. With her audacious spirit, she put it this way, "I'm a woman, I'm colored, I'm big. That's who I am." She began her performing career as a singer but switched to acting, making her motion picture debut in 1931. Responding to charges of accepting subservient roles, McDaniel made the now famous remark, "I'd rather play a maid for $700 per week than to be one for $7 per week." Her credo may have been "one has to go along to get along" because she is said to have cautioned fellow actress Butterfly McQueen (Prissy in *Gone with the Wind*), "You'll never come back to Hollywood, you complain too much."

About the role of Mammy in *Gone with the Wind*, McDaniel said, "I tried to make her a living, breathing character . . . to glorify Negro womanhood; not the modern, streamline type of Negro woman who attends teas and concerts in ermine and mink, but the type of Negro of the period which gave us Harriet Tubman, Sojourner Truth" In scene after scene, McDaniel displayed a full range of histrionic skills, from her own brand of comedy to deep pathos and grief. With an authority and toughness unique among house slaves, Mammy orders other slaves around and berates black soldiers when they appear to threaten Scarlett. After the war, Mammy rejects freedom in favor of remaining Scarlett's loyal servant. McDaniel claimed that Mammy was Scarlett O'Hara's conscience when Scarlett had none.

Mammy exhorts Scarlett not to "act like 'po' white trash chillun,' taint fittin.'" McDaniel's comic capability is always evident. When Scarlett proceeds to get drunk on brandy following the death of her husband of convenience, Mammy delivers with deadpan accuracy the line, "Miz Scarlett, Captain Butler's here to see you. I told him you was prostrate with grief."

Gone with the Wind premiered at the Loew's Grand Theater in Atlanta on December 14, 1939. Hattie McDaniel and the film's other black actors were not invited because of Georgia's segregation laws at the time. The Ebenezer Baptist Church choir appeared dressed in slave costumes in keeping with the film's era. It is said that a ten-year-old Martin Luther King Jr. was one of the child singers. Resentment abounded from blacks upset by the film's subtext that Southern blacks did little more during the Civil War than worry about the fate of Miz Scarlett and Massa Rhett. Hattie confided to Hollywood columnist Louella Parsons, "I love Mammy. I think I understand her because my own grandmother worked on a plantation not unlike Tara." Criticism from the NAACP did bring about some concessions, such as the deletion of *nigger* from the dialogue.

In 1936 the Academy of Motion Picture Arts and Sciences expanded the categories eligible for awards to include supporting role performances. Three years later, Hattie McDaniel became not only the first ever African American actor to be nominated for an award but the first to win one.

The Academy Award ceremony took place at the Coconut Grove of the Ambassador Hotel in Los Angeles on February 29, 1940. Hattie was the first African American attendee at an Academy banquet. She was relegated to sitting with her escort at a rear table away from the Caucasian attendees, but Hattie was too much the consummate professional to complain. She accepted the Oscar from actress Fay Bainter. Adorned with gardenias, McDaniel conveyed her unmistakable joy, "This is the happiest moment of my life, it makes me feel very humble and I shall always hold it as a beacon for anything that I may be able to do in the future. I sincerely hope that I shall be a credit to my race and to the motion picture industry. Thank you." As McDaniel left the microphone, she burst into tears, overcome by the honor.

Some civil rights activists who had protested the filming of Margaret Mitchell's blatantly pro-Confederate best-seller urged Hattie to decline the award. Such a symbolic gesture was completely unprecedented in an era well before the controversial rejections of Oscars by actors Marlon Brando and George C. Scott.

Over the years, there have been various accounts concerning actress Olivia de Havilland's reaction to losing to McDaniel. Playing Melanie, one of the four lead characters in *Gone with the Wind*, Olivia was inappropriately nominated in the supporting role category when in reality she was one of the film's stars. Upon hearing the name of the winner, Olivia rushed, weeping, from the table of Selznick (producer of the film) into the kitchen. Mrs. Selznick followed, attempting to reason with her and forseeing that a young Olivia would have other chances for an Oscar in the future, while this would probably be Hattie's one and only shot. The prediction proved to be true when Olivia de Havilland subsequently won Oscars for leading roles in *To Each His Own* (1946) and *The Heiress* (1949). De Havilland in retrospect recalls the incident as a learning experience. Weeks after the ceremony she realized how proud she was to belong to a profession that honored a black woman of merit at a time when other groups had neither the honesty nor the courage to do so.

The Oscar won by Hattie seems to have developed a life of its own. Hattie's generosity prompted her to lend it briefly to an esteemed black stage actress, Mercedes Gilbert. Then in 1952, following Hattie's death, it was bequeathed to Howard University. The statuette seems to have disappeared from the university sometime in the 1960s.

In 1975 Hattie McDaniel was admitted posthumously into the Black Filmmakers Hall of Fame.

As recently as 1999, her legend was alive and well. *Hi Hat Hattie*, written by Larry Parr and introduced in 1991, was still being performed around the country. The one-woman show with music covers McDaniel's career as a radio singer as well as a film actress. Six decades after she won an Oscar and five decades after her death, the new owners of Hollywood Memorial Park Cemetery (renamed Hollywood Forever) have installed a pink granite memorial stone in remembrance of the first black Oscar winner, whose wish was to be buried there. The cemetery did not accept blacks when McDaniel died in 1952 and refused her interment.

1946

James Baskett

b. *February 16, 1904, Indianapolis, Indiana*
d. *July 9, 1948, Los Angeles, California*

Recipient, Special Oscar 1946
UNCLE REMUS in *Song of the South*

The Academy of Motion Picture Arts and Sciences presented James Baskett with a special award in 1947 "for his able and heart-warming characterization of Uncle Remus, friend and storyteller to the children of the world." Legendary Hollywood columnist Hedda Hopper lobbied to make the special award happen. Baskett died the following year.

Set on a Southern plantation, the film shows the close relationship between a black antebellum Uncle Remus and a little white boy to whom he tells stories and sings while colorful birds perch on his shoulder, visualized by Disney animation. The composer and lyricist of the theme "Zip-a-Dee-Doo-Dah" took home an Oscar for best song. One line of the song refers to "everything being satisfactual," which was hardly the case as far as the NAACP was concerned. That organization vocalized its concern about the exploitation of the beloved Uncle Remus character as a tool for stereotyping the African American image on film.

Having tested Baskett for a minor role earlier, Disney remembered the actor and subsequently signed him for the part of Uncle Remus. For many years, Baskett was a member of the Lafayette Players, a premier African American theatrical repertory company in Harlem. In the 1930s, he did a vaudeville turn at the famed Apollo Theater with other "race film" players. The skits performed would often coincide with the screening of a separate (racially segregated) film like *Policy*

Man, in which he appeared with musician Count Basie under the name Jimmie Baskette. Baskett was also known for the role of Gabby Gibson, a slick-talking lawyer on radio's *Amos 'n' Andy* program. Like *Gone with the Wind, Song of the South* premiered in Atlanta. Unlike the other black actors in the film who were unwelcome, Baskett did not even try to attend because of illness.

More than a half century after the film's original release, the Disney organization still has not made it available on video. Its story and characterizations might be deemed politically incorrect by a new generation of viewers. Currently the film is available only on Japanese import laserdisc. Those who favor the film see it merely as a whimsical folk tale and therefore not an impediment to racial healing; those who disagree consider it as unabashed, antebellum, Uncle Tom foolery.

A final and humorous note occurred during the Clinton White House scandal when a musical revue poked fun at the president. It titled its version of the Uncle Remus song: "Unzippin' My Doodah."

1949

Ethel Waters

b. *October 21, 1896, Chester, Pennsylvania*
d. *September 1, 1977, Los Angeles, California*

Nominee, Best Supporting Actress, 1949
DICEY JOHNSON in *Pinky*

Following her starring role in MGM's *Cabin in the Sky* (1943), work in motion pictures no longer came for Ethel Waters. She may have won her internecine battles on the set of *Cabin*, but she most certainly had lost the war. Before being contacted by Twentieth Century Fox to test for a part in a John Ford film (he was later replaced as director by Elia Kazan), Waters had been living in virtual isolation at a friend's home in Harlem. Capturing the role of Dicey Johnson in *Pinky*, based on Cid Sumner's novel *Quality*, recharged Waters's then flagging career, bringing her meaty character roles in films like *Member of the Wedding* (1952) and *The Sound and the Fury* (1959). *Pinky* was not the first film about racial passing to achieve widespread attention. In 1934, *Imitation of Life*, featuring Louise Beavers and Fredi Washington, had dealt with the same explosive topic, as adapted from Fannie Hurst's novel. While *Pinky* brought a supporting actress nomination for Waters, Beavers received none because the Academy did not recognize supporting role performances until 1936. In 1949, Mercedes McCambridge took home an Oscar for *All the King's Men*, defeating both Ethels (Waters and Barrymore) for their work in *Pinky*.

Waters's character Dicey Johnson reprises an all-too-familiar image in American films, bandana wearing, devoutly religious, and an always-faithful servant. She does washing without pay for Miss Em (Ethel Barrymore), a sick elderly aristocrat. Most of Dicey's dialogue is with God, not with the other characters. When her granddaughter

Pinky returns from the North, where she was passing, Dicey insists that Pinky nurse the cantankerous white woman. Convinced that her own faith has brought about the return of her granddaughter, Dicey advises Pinky that passing is a sin before God: "denying yo' self like Peter denied the Lord." She insists Pinky get on her knees and ask forgiveness for her sins. Later Dicey is seen, not unexpectedly, at the foot of Miss Em's death bed, praying. Her simple credo is expressed: "If they is somethin' white folks don't want you to have or somethin' they want fo' theyself, you might as well forget all about it." Dicey wants Pinky to know her place as a Negro; she wants to mold Pinky in her own image.

Pinky was one of several Hollywood-produced "problem flicks" to emerge at about the same time during a pseudoliberal postwar period. The others were *Intruder in the Dust*, *Home of the Brave*, and *Lost Boundaries*, all in 1949, followed by *No Way Out* in 1950. Some Southern cities banned *Pinky*, which led to a Supreme Court case that overturned the censorship, extending first amendment protection to films.

Ethel Waters once remarked, "I hate to sing. I do it for a living. I'd rather act." Years later, when she became a major figure in Reverend Billy Graham's evangelical crusades, her joy in singing was reclaimed, but that singing was devoted exclusively to sacred music.

1954

Dorothy Dandridge

b. *November 9, 1922, Cleveland, Ohio*
d. *September 8, 1965, Los Angeles, California*

Nominee, Best Actress, 1954
CARMEN JONES in *Carmen Jones*

Dorothy Dandridge had made several film appearances over the years in low-budget films, in small roles in mainstream films, and in larger roles for "race movies," but *Carmen Jones* was her biggest break. James Edwards (*Home of the Brave*, 1949) was enlisted to assist Dandridge in her test for the role of Carmen. Although he was not going to play opposite her as Joe (Harry Belafonte had been cast), Edwards brought his special charisma to the now famous toenail polishing scene, complementing Dorothy's seductive excitement with his own brand of sexual appeal. Once Dorothy was signed for *Carmen,* few people knew that she had seriously considered backing out. Since she had struggled so tenaciously to win the part, her interim decision not to do *Carmen* was unquestionably prompted by the insecurity and low self-esteem that plagued her for her entire life.

James Baldwin in his *Notes of a Native Son* writes, "The most important thing about the movie—and the reason that, despite itself, it is one of the most important all-Negro movies Hollywood has yet produced—is that the questions it leaves in the mind relate less to Negroes than to the interior life of Americans."

On March 30, 1955, Dandridge attended the Oscar ceremony at the Century Theater in New York City, because she had nightclub engagements to fulfill at New York's Waldorf Astoria. The press was abuzz with Dorothy's chances of winning, almost as though it were a sports event. *Jet* magazine wrote, "The latest Hollywood report being circulated: This year's Oscar race may be the biggest upset in history. People are betting Dorothy Dandridge will cop the award." Otto Preminger, the film's director, admitted that she deserved the trophy, but he doubted that the time and racial climate were right. When William Holden in Hollywood announced Grace Kelly the winner for *The Country Girl*, Dandridge displayed a facade of good sportsmanship, but everyone felt that not only her dream but the dream of African Americans was once again being deferred. It should be noted that Kelly's award was for a much-heralded drama, whereas best acting awards rarely went to a performance in a musical. As black film historian Donald Bogle so aptly notes, "For a black performer in fifties Hollywood, being nominated for the Oscar was tantamount to actually winning the award."

With the exception of *Island in the Sun* (1957), *Porgy and Bess* (1959), and a few pictures made in Europe, Dorothy's career and early promise had ended. The Hollywood film industry appeared reluctant and confused as to how to showcase Dorothy's unique assets. It is clear they had no clue as to why a lovely and talented actress on tour would carry around a trunk with fine linen tablecloths and silver place settings—so that, should she wish to have dinner guests, she need not worry about being rejected in a top restaurant. Actress Halle Berry who starred in the 1990 HBO drama *Introducing Dorothy Dandridge* gained some retrospective insight into the frustration of Dandridge four decades earlier as she herself researched and prepared to play Dandridge.

Depressed and bankrupt, Dandridge died of a drug overdose in 1965, shortly after her 43rd birthday. Correctly, she has been described as an individual whose legacy of courage lives on and as a pioneer who possessed the strength to achieve.

1958

Sidney Poitier

b. February 20, 1927, Miami, Florida

Nominee, Best Actor, 1958
NOAH CULLEN in *The Defiant Ones*

The film's plot chronicles the manhunt for two fugitives from a Southern chain gang who are shackled to each other. In a feeble effort to obfuscate an integrationist message, Poitier's character is made to save Tony Curtis's character from drowning while confiding, "I didn't pull you out, I kept you from pulling me in." The two characters symbolize the outcasts of our society linked together in their struggle against the established order, a metaphor strengthened visually because one is black and the other white. The film allowed, for the first time, a black and white actor to interact on an equal basis. A particularly memorable moment of the film occurs as Poitier, holding the white man in his arms, bellows defiantly the old blues number "Long Gone," a possible precursor of his rendition of "Amen" in *Lilies of the Field*, five years later. The final scene of the movie sometimes evokes derision from today's viewers. The late black comedian Godfrey Cambridge satirized the moment in which Poitier jumps from a moving freight train, sacrificing his own freedom for Tony Curtis, who has fallen behind. In theaters, white audiences approved, but black audiences shouted to Sidney, "Get back on the train!" Cambridge joked, "A real black brother would have remained on the train bidding raucous farewell to the white man with 'Bye! Baby.'"

Stanley Kramer, the film's director, said, "Poitier is the only actor I've ever worked with who has the range of Marlon Brando—from pathos to great power. Like Brando, he can be a pathetic and even pitiful character, and then he can go instantly to moments of overwhelming and savage emotional power."

Poitier's chances of carrying off a best actor Academy Award for his role as an escaped convict were probably diminished by the fact that his costar, Tony Curtis, had been nominated in the same category. Actually it was Tony Curtis who had insisted that then little-known Poitier be granted equal billing above the title. The Oscar went to David Niven for his understated performance in *Separate Tables*, wiping out his two competitors from *The Defiant Ones*. Starring on Broadway in *A Raisin in the Sun*, Poitier did not attend the Oscar ceremony. Although the film won no Oscar for Poitier or Curtis, it did receive awards for best story and best screenplay, as well as for best black and white cinematography. Poitier fared better in Germany, where Eleanor Roosevelt presented him with the Berlin Film Festival's Golden Bear as best actor for *The Defiant Ones*.

Hollywood seems compelled to replicate its successes. In 1973, *The Defiant Ones* theme was attempted with a gender change. Pam Grier and her white female costar are shackled together as they run from the law in *Black Mama, White Mama*. About a dozen years later, Carl Weathers took the Poitier role in a 1985 television version. Regretfully, Hollywood seems unable to resist equating white racism with black defiance, refusing to recognize the cause/effect relationship between the two behaviors. Nowhere is this point clearer than in the 1997 *Amistad*, which graphically depicts black violence but merely suggests the white brutality that instigates it.

1959

Juanita Moore

b. October 19, 1922, Los Angeles, California

Nominee, Best Supporting Actress, 1959
ANNIE JOHNSON in *Imitation of Life*

Educated in Los Angeles, Juanita Moore first considered an acting career on the advice of a teacher at Jefferson High School. She was later inspired by performances of the Lafayette Players, a popular black theater group that was appearing in Los Angeles. She studied at the Actors' Lab in Hollywood, where she met a young Marlon Brando. Work with the Ebony Showcase Theater followed. This group provided black actors like Beah Richards, James Edwards, and Moore a chance to do nonstereotypical work denied them in film.

Other African American actresses (including Pearl Bailey) were considered by producer Ross Hunter and director Douglas Sirk to play Annie. Fortunately Sirk pushed successfully for Moore. She is eternally grateful to him not only for helping her land the role but for encouraging her throughout filming. This role had garnered praise for actress Louise Beavers in the original 1934 film. Moore's response to winning the role was, "To me this is the break every actress dreams of getting." Dealing with issues of race and gender, the plot concerns two single mothers—one white (Lana Turner), one black (Moore)—rearing their respective daughters. The black woman's light complexioned and truculent daughter tries to pass for white, bringing sorrow and shame to her mother, who has become Turner's selfless maid. Annie is gentle with her white employer's daughter but stern with her own black child. When Sarah Jane becomes an adult, she refuses to embrace the perpetual humiliation that she believes defines her mother Annie's life. That the story is artificial and contrived was even more evident in 1959 than it had been in 1934, fresh from Fannie Hurst's novel and its serialization in *Cosmopolitan* as "Sugar House." In a prolonged deathbed sequence, Moore's character, Annie, has to breathe life into this saccharin dialogue: "Tell her [the absent daughter played by Susan Kohner] I know I was selfish and if I loved her too much, I'm sorry but I didn't mean to cause her any trouble. She was all I had." Annie is a born martyr who dies exhausted, sad, and accepting of the status quo in an almost masochistic way. Although, for a time, the film was the most commercially successful Universal had ever made, critics labeled it "almost unbelievably ridiculous" and "the wettest wallow in cheap sentiment that Hollywood has sent us for years." But even one negative review disclaims, "only the superior performance of Juanita Moore keeps it [the film] alive." The marquee at the famed Apollo Theater in Harlem read "*Imitation of Life* Starring Juanita Moore." Moore mused, "Lana would have a fit if she saw that."

Juanita Moore lost the best supporting actress Oscar to Shelley Winters for *The Diary of Anne Frank*. Since Susan Kohner was also nominated in the same category, it is safe to assume that the two actresses from *Imitation of Life* diminished each other's chances for a win. One could easily view the pivotal role of Annie as leading, not supporting, but even the Academy admits the acting categories can be arbitrary. Robert Rehme, recent Academy President, states, "There is a book of rules but they don't really mean anything. The nominations are based largely on where the studios choose to place them." With his leading lady, Doris Day, also up for an Oscar for *Pillow Talk*, producer Ross Hunter did little to advance Moore's nomination, distributing the studio's biography of her to the media only at the eleventh hour. Despite Moore's key role in the film, closing credits speak volumes about the segregated status of black actors in the pre–Civil Rights Era. The entire cast is listed, including the smallest roles. At the very end of the list, we observe "Juanita Moore as Annie and Mahalia Jackson as choir singer," not set off from the rest of the cast as sometimes done for special circumstances.

Comedian Richard Pryor recalls a painful personal incident associated with the film while he was stationed in Germany as an enlisted soldier. A racially motivated fracus ensued when a young white soldier laughed inappropriately at the tragic plight of the film's two black characters.

After her Academy Award nomination, work remained scarce for Moore. Almost immediately following her role in *Imitation of Life*, the actress journeyed to London, where she performed the matriarch role of Lena Younger in *A Raisin in the Sun* for a stage production in the West End. More recently, Moore has rechanneled her employment frustration by teaching acting classes at the Ebony Showcase Theater to low-income students in the Los Angeles community. This organization gave many prominent actors, including Moore, their first professional experience, consequently broadening the images of black Americans in film and television as well as theater.

Early in 2000, accompanying her grandson (an aspiring actor) to an agent interview, Moore was rediscovered. That incident led to her work in Disney's *The Kid*.

1963

Sidney Poitier

b. February 20, 1927, Miami, Florida

Winner, Best Actor, 1963
HOMER SMITH in *Lilies of the Field*

Sidney Poitier has been called the Jackie Robinson of American film, and with good reason. He entered Hollywood films when opportunities for actors of color were nonexistent. Although Poitier was born in the United States he remains a citizen of the Bahamas, birthplace of his parents. A small shoebox to serve as a coffin was acquired in 1927 for the three-pound infant, who was not expected to live. Nevertheless a local seer predicted he would not only survive but travel the world over and walk with kings. Seventy years later Poitier became the Bahamas' ambassador to Japan, presenting his credentials to the emperor at a formal ceremony in Tokyo. This honor was accompanied by an office in Nassau to facilitate the fulfillment of his ambassadorial duties.

While Poitier had made numerous films prior to 1963, *Lilies of the Field* was destined to become his vehicle to the Oscar. Harry Belafonte claims that he was offered the role but turned it down, as he deemed the character a nonperson. The story was adapted for the screen by Ralph Nelson from a novella by W. E. Barrett. The cast rehearsed at the director Nelson's home in California before going on location to Arizona for the shoot, which was completed in two weeks at less than $500,000.

The plot introduces Poitier as Homer Smith, a former G.I. who, drifting westward, encounters some East German nuns in an Arizona desert mission house. Homer is described in racially free

23

terms despite his obvious color. The nuns are refugees from behind the Soviet iron curtain. Against his initial impulse, the itinerant handyman is cajoled into building them a much-needed chapel. The tension and confrontations between Homer and the forceful but lovable Mother Superior give the film its energy. A highlight of the film is Homer's scene instructing the nuns in singing "Amen." The popular song was dubbed by the late Jester Hairston, a revered veteran African American singer/actor. Director Nelson came up with a television adaptation (*Christmas Lilies of the Field*, with Billy Dee Williams) in 1970, which was followed by a commercially unsuccessful stage version (*Look to the Lilies*) in 1979.

That Poitier's Academy nomination came in the midst of the civil rights struggle did not go unnoticed by the press. Sidney Skolsky wrote, "If ever there was a year when the Negro be honored it is this year for obvious reasons. It should pour soothing oil on the troubled racial waters and, besides, it is deserved. It would also telegraph to the globe that we do not discriminate." Although winning seemed a long shot, Poitier vacillated from a "no chance at all" stance to drafting an acceptance speech. When actress Anne Bancroft called his name on April 13, 1964, the actor vaguely remembers leaping out of his seat, heading for the stage with great strides, hugging Bancroft and grasping the statuette. Poitier recalls looking out at the thousands of applauding people in the Santa Monica Civic Auditorium. By the time the applause had subsided, Poitier, close to tears, had regained his composure and began, "It is a long journey to this moment. I am naturally indebted to countless numbers of people. To them, all I can say is a very special thank you." For the record, his emotional remarks were the epitome of brevity. To this very day, he sees the Oscar as a symbol of accomplishment in a very exact discipline.

Weeks after the Oscar ceremony, Poitier returned to a tremendous welcome in Nassau. Not even Bahamas rain could mar the celebration. Signs proclaimed: "HAIL SIDNEY, GREATEST ACTOR IN THE WORLD," "WELCOME HOME SIDNEY," "WE ADORE YOU SIDNEY," and "YOUR GLORY IS OURS." The Berlin Film Festival also accorded Sidney the best actor award for the film. Many more honors were yet to come.

On June 23, 1967 Poitier had his hand- and footprints set in cement at Hollywood's Grauman's Chinese Theater, additional validation of his admission to the permanent history of the film industry. Five years after his Oscar win, Poitier was declared the U.S. box office champion in 1968 because of the successes of his three 1967 films: *Guess Who's Coming to Dinner?*, *To Sir, With Love*, and *In the Heat of the Night*. Ironically, he did not receive an Academy nomination for any one of these three films. Thirty years later, the Academy did pay special tribute to the actor with a program at its Samuel Goldwyn Theater featuring speeches by those who shared experiences with this screen giant, backed up with clips from some of his memorable films. The Screen Actors Guild selected Poitier as the 36th recipient of its Life Achievement Award for an Outstanding Career and Humanitarian Accomplishment. The American Film Institute named Poitier one of the 50 (25 male, 25 female) greatest screen legends. As the only African American on the list, he placed at number 22. To be eligible actors had to make a screen debut in or before 1950 which just qualified Poitier on the basis of his debut film *No Way Out* in 1950.

In the 1970s, Sidney turned to directing films (*Buck and the Preacher*, *Stir Crazy*, *Uptown Saturday Night*, et al) Following some years behind the camera, he reappeared on screen, now as an older featured actor in such films as *Shoot to Kill* and *Little Nikita*.

Fellow African American artists have paid personal tribute to Sidney. Morgan Freeman declaimed, "I speak for two generations of black actors when I thank you, Mr. Poitier, for sticking to your dream, for in so doing you've set fire to mine." John Singleton referred to Poitier as "a pioneer who changed the way African Americans are regarded on the screen." James Earl Jones remarked, "Sidney invented the African American in film. He invented it and then he perfected it." Sidney himself stated, "It was never impossible; it was harder." This utterance was from the first major African American film star whose crossover allowed people to identify with him regardless of color, a man who literally changed the complexion of movies.

Accepting an honorary Oscar at the 74th annual Academy Awards Ceremony, Poitier payed tribute to the "memory of all the African American actors and actresses who went before me in the difficult years." For those unfamiliar with films in the pre-Poitier era, this was a clear reference to performers such as Hattie McDaniel, Paul Robeson, and Canada Lee among others. In this the twenty-first century, Sidney Poitier does not see himself retired either as actor or director.

1967

Beah Richards

b. July 12, 1920, Vicksburg, Mississippi
d. September 14, 2000, Vicksburg, Mississippi

Nominee, Best Supporting Actress, 1967
MRS. PRENTICE in *Guess Who's Coming to Dinner?*

Beah Richards was one of the few black actresses who consistently refused to accept roles that were racially demeaning and exploitative.

Guess Who's Coming to Dinner? unveils the reactions of an upscale but liberal Caucasian couple (Spencer Tracy, Katherine Hepburn) when their only daughter announces her intention to wed a black man (Sidney Poitier), who just happens to be an internationally known doctor, a combination of Albert Schweitzer and Charles Drew in the persona of Sidney Poitier. Richards plays his mother, who is shocked initially that her son has chosen to marry a white woman. Audiences expect her to release her obviously repressed emotions over the situation but she remains superficially placid. Her respectable middle-class reserve tips the audience that she will support her son's decision ultimately. Richards enjoyed working with Tracy, Hepburn, and Poitier, "an opportunity I think I will treasure most of my life." The movie became the second-highest grosser of the year, hard on the tail of Mike Nichols' *The Graduate*. Even though one critic termed the film, "a styrofoam soaper," it made the official list of America's One Hundred Greatest Movies selected by the American Film Institute. Selections were made by a blue ribbon panel of more than fifteen hundred leaders of the American movie community. Richards enjoyed a harvest year in 1967, with three successful films playing in motion picture theaters around the country. In addition to *Guess Who's Coming to Dinner?* there was *Hurry Sundown* and *In the*

Heat of the Night, in which she also worked with Poitier. He correctly believed that Richards "lived in a time that was not prepared to explore all the dimensions of her gifts, she was underused."

The Oscar ceremony, scheduled originally for April 9, 1968, the day of Martin Luther King Jr.'s funeral, was held a day later out of respect for the slain civil rights leader. Several film stars, including Sidney Poitier, Diahann Carroll, and Sammy Davis Jr., had petitioned the Academy for a postponement. The popular song classic "The Glory of Love"—with its lyric "You've got to win a little, lose a little"—used as *Guess Who's Coming to Dinner?*'s musical theme, probably resonated with Richards, who lost the Oscar to Estelle Parsons for *Bonnie and Clyde*.

Three years later, Richards was cast as James Earl Jones's mother in *The Great White Hope*. She once said jokingly, "I have played everybody's mother." Three decades after her Academy nomination, Beah Richards played Baby Suggs in *Beloved*, giving a striking performance that combined authority, exhortation, and mysticism. In 2000 she won an Emmy for a guest role performance on the hit television series *The Practice*. Too ill to travel to Los Angeles to receive the award, Richards commented from her home in Vicksburg, Mississippi, "They made this the experience of a lifetime for this old lady."

A multitalented professional, Richards was a writer as well as an actress. Among the books she produced are *A Black Woman Speaks* (1964) and *One Is a Crowd* (1970). A measure of her perception and intellectual grasp may be seen in her own words, "Both class and race survive education, and neither should. What is education then if it doesn't allow a human being to recognize that humanity is humanity, what is it for? So you can make a bigger salary than other people?" This was Beah Richards.

1969

Rupert Crosse

b. 1927, New York, New York
d. March 5, 1973, Nevis, West Indies

Nominee, Best Supporting Actor, 1969
NED MCCASLIN in *The Reivers*

The Reivers (Scottish for *robbers*) should not be categorized with the cycle of films in the late 1960s dealing with racial prejudice. Its theme is universal; it is based on William Faulkner's novel of the same name. The film was also known as *Yellow Winton Flyer*. Rupert Crosse played Ned McCaslin, a raffish but congenial black stable hand who accompanies the main characters, portrayed by Steve McQueen and Mitch Vogel, on an adventurous trip from Jefferson, Mississippi, to Memphis, Tennessee, in 1905 behind the wheel of a rare, prized yellow Winton Flyer. Ned is enthralled by a beautiful racehorse (symbolically black) that is noted for its reluctance to race. Ned discovers the secret to overcoming the thoroughbred's flaw (a love of sardines). A conveniently truthful bit of Southern history lets the audience in on the fact that Ned has the same great granddad as a white livery stable owner. This revelation explains perhaps why Ned does not seem bound by the usual code of a segregated society. One critic credited Crosse with "making the screen more interesting whenever he was on it." Initially McQueen, who was seeking a little guy for the part, didn't want to cast Crosse because his impressive six-foot-five appearance might pilfer attention.

Crosse, who became the first black actor to garner an Academy Award nomination in a supporting role, lost to Gig Young, a previous nominee, who won for *They Shoot Horses, Don't They?* Young's actual star stint received a supporting nomination, which compromised Crosse's chance of winning. The increasingly common phenomenon of interchanging lead and support categories is unfortunate, in that it prevents those who actually perform supporting roles from having a real shot at the Oscar.

Rupert Crosse would have undoubtedly achieved wider and greater recognition had lung cancer not claimed him at the untimely age of forty-five on the island of Nevis.

Almost three decades later, Crosse was remembered publicly by Jack Nicholson as he accepted his third Oscar. Paying a touching tribute to several individuals, Rupert Crosse among them, Nicholson declared, "They're not here anymore but they're in my heart."

1970

James Earl Jones

b. January 17, 1931, Arkabutla, Mississippi

Nominee, Best Actor, 1970
JACK JEFFERSON in *The Great White Hope*

James Earl Jones, who created the role of Jack Jefferson on the Broadway stage, was unenthusiastic about elements of the film production of *The Great White Hope*, including a change in director from Ed Sherin to Martin Ritt and a shift toward the "larger-than-life" nature of some of the characters. He believed that much of the poetry and passion of the play had been eliminated. The actor, who hung out with Muhammad Ali as part of his preparation for the role, wondered why the script did not include more boxing. Was there a subconscious effort to emasculate the heroic figure of the champion? Much of the filming was done on location in Barcelona with English-speaking personnel.

In reviewing Jones's performance, *Time* acclaimed, "It is the kind of pounding, feinting, bloody, unbowing portrayal that insures an Academy award nomination and possibly the prize itself." This prediction was at least half right. Disappointed in his own performance and the overall quality of the film, Jones expected the Oscar to go to George C. Scott. Indeed the Oscar race became a duel between the characterizations of a champion pugilist and a famed military hero. At the end of the day, Jones did lose to Scott for his role as Patton, a victory that was underscored by Scott's rejection of the statuette. Calling the ceremony a "meat parade," Scott charged that it was offensive, barbarous, and innately corrupt for actors to compete against one another.

Success does not necessarily offer black actors even the few bene-fits afforded white actors of comparable status. Approximately a decade after his Oscar nomination, Jones was required to audition for a small role in *Ragtime,* a part that ultimately went to Moses Gunn. Actor Samuel L. Jackson summarized the situation with telling accu-racy, "You either want James Earl Jones for a part or you don't." If James Earl Jones's ubiquitous television spots on behalf of a certain telephone company are any indication, he is very much wanted.

1972

Diana Ross

b. *March 26, 1944, Detroit, Michigan*

Nominee, Best Actress, 1972
BILLIE HOLIDAY in *Lady Sings the Blues*

Having acted before only once, briefly, as a nun in an episode of
Tarzan on television, singer Diana Ross entered unexplored terri-
tory with the role of Billie Holiday. Initially, jazz singer Abbey Lincoln had been considered for the role, but she had to decline. Being cast as the legendary blues singer presented Ross with the
challenge of her career. It was quite a showcase for her motion picture debut, and Ross met the undertaking admirably. In the role,
she alternates as required between vulnerable, hysterical, sensi-
tive, and tempestuous. Posters for the film proclaimed, "Diana
Ross Is Billie Holiday." Many who knew "Lady Day" disagreed,
but conceded that Hollywood technicolor musical biographies are
rarely models of reality. Some felt the script and portrayal lacked
the hard-hitting strength and raw nerve delineated in the book.
Diana's best work was in the drug scenes. Ross admits, "I was surprised how good I was." Queried about exactly what aspect of her
personal life she drew upon to evoke the pathos and disintegra-
tion she brought to the screen, Ross replied, "It's a secret." *Rolling
Stone* magazine really gushed over the portrayal, citing, "each
flutter of those heavy lids" and "each shrug of those exquisite
shoulders" as proof positive of Diana's total immersion in the
role. Ross is among those few actresses singled out for a nomination by the Academy in a film debut. Another was Whoopi Goldberg for *The Color Purple* in 1985.

Diana Ross lost the Oscar to Liza Minelli for *Cabaret*. Minelli at one point in the proceedings thought Ross was the winner, and not just out of respect for Diana's work. It seems Ross had changed the dress she was wearing moments before the announcement of the best actress award, as if she knew something was about to happen. Some thought Ross lost to Minelli because Motown had tried too hard in pushing her for the award. A massive print campaign was mounted, lauding Ross's performance, which sometimes engenders a backlash. Berry Gordy bought full-page ads on a regular basis showing photos of Ross in various, even sordid, scenes from the film, which might have struck some Academy members as overkill. It was rumored that Diana's new poodle had been named, conveniently, "Oscar." Following this important nomination the career of Diana Ross moved in a different direction. Her film career culminated with first the role of elegant fashion designer in *Mahogany* (1975) and later that of Dorothy in the musical *The Wiz* (1978). Since then, Diana Ross has concentrated on recordings and concerts. Not every singer who forays into motion pictures emerges as a major screen star.

1972

Cicely Tyson

b. December 19, 1933, New York, New York

Nominee, Best Actress, 1972
REBECCA MORGAN in *Sounder*

Speaking of her role in *Sounder,* Cicely Tyson stated, "Rebecca is the first positive portrayal of a black woman on the screen. Always before, she has been a con woman, a prostitute, a drug addict. The time has come for blacks to look back at our history and be proud of it and not ashamed." Tyson patterned the part of Rebecca after her mother as well as after the woman who took care of her while her mother worked. Rebecca is a stoic sharecropper's wife in a segregated Louisiana during the Depression Era. A black woman had not been seen previously on screen as such a symbol of pride, dignity, love, strength, and courage in the face of enormous adversity.

No African American actress had been nominated in the best actress in a leading role category since the first one, Dorothy Dandridge, eighteen years earlier. The year 1972 brought two such nominations, Tyson and Diana Ross for *Lady Sings the Blues,* each most probably canceling out the other's chance to win. Tyson reveled in her nomination: "I'm proud and I want every person in the world to see the film . . . in a year in which Diana Ross is also a nominee, it is a double honor."

Lonne Elder III also received a nomination for best screenplay. *Sounder* was based on William Armstrong's novel, in which the family's race is not mentioned. Elder's adaptation is especially noteworthy for its poignant dialogue.

Responses to *Sounder* were anything but unanimous, with vocalizations coming from both the pro and the con camps.

Vincent Canby of the *New York Times* was not among those to sing *Sounder*'s praises. He stated, "*Sounder* is the sort of movie that patronizes the 'littleness' of its characters, that makes even sweat look fake and that asks its audience to say 'aw-w-w-w' when the faithful old dog comes limping out of the woods licking its wounds." African American author Lindsay Patterson challenged the authenticity of a mother (Rebecca) who does not grow her own vegetable garden to feed her family, a criticism that could be seen as nitpicking. Other justifiably cynical blacks viewed with some suspicion a film that reassures whites who want to believe that blacks react to racism with love, trust, and obedience as opposed to rage and bitterness.

Tyson was lauded for her ability to convey emotion such as joy or discouragement through her eyes and her posture, given the fact that she had a dearth of dialogue. Among those appreciative of Tyson's portrayal was Beah Richards, Oscar nominee for best supporting actress in 1967. She broke into tears and threw her arms around Tyson after viewing the film, exclaiming, "I cannot tell you what you have done for black women." Tyson herself acknowledged, "I know there may never be a part like Rebecca in *Sounder* again . . . and if that's the case, I may just have to hang up my gloves." Fortunately for audiences everywhere Cicely Tyson is still very much in the game.

1972

Paul Winfield

b. May 22, 1941, Los Angeles, California

Nominee, Best Actor, 1972
NATHAN LEE MORGAN in *Sounder*

Some African Americans were upset with the portrayal of Nathan Lee Morgan as a man submissive to racial injustice meted out by a bigoted sheriff. Black author Lindsay Patterson calls into question why a long-suffering father (Nathan Lee) living under oppressive circumstances does not get on a train and seek a friendlier environment elsewhere. Furthermore, Patterson feels it requires no stretch of the imagination to understand Hollywood's praise of a film that almost canonizes a docile masochistic black. On the other hand, Winfield sees anachronism: "We owe it to our parents and grandparents to make accurate movies of their lives and struggles. The fight for civil rights did not begin in the late 1950s. . . . It began with them. From their frustrations the civil rights movement grew." With this in mind, Winfield could see the film as the real black experience. *Sounder* was seen by many as a welcome alternative to the black exploitation plots involving guns, drugs, sex, and gratuitous violence. Criticizing the "blaxploitation" movies of the 1970s, Paul Winfield commented, "Those cats don't show any humor or emotion. They just get in and out of bed." Lacking in quality, blaxploitation films were destined for a short life, notwithstanding the fact that they provided unprecedented employment for black actors.

Kevin Hooks, who played Nathan Lee's young son in *Sounder*, recalls naively asking Martin Ritt, the director, "This is the kind of film that gets nominated for Academy Awards, right?" Ritt replied, "No, this is the kind of film that never gets nominated for Academy Awards. It's too small and it's too personal." Happily, a short time later Ritt was proven wrong.

Without doubt *Sounder*'s most memorable moment is when sharecropper Nathan Lee, jailed for stealing food for his wife and son, returns home, limping along, as his tearful wife Rebecca races to greet him. This scene alone explains the nominations of Winfield and Tyson. Although Winfield lost to Marlon Brando for his role in *The Godfather*, a blockbuster, Paul took special pride in his nomination, for he was vying with heady competition. The actor believed that even though he lost the Oscar, he already had won. His achievement of a nomination as best actor in a leading role performance by an African American actor was only the third in Academy history.

1974

Diahann Carroll

b. June 17, 1935, New York, New York

Nominee, Best Actress, 1974
CLAUDINE PRICE in *Claudine*

The incredibly talented actress Diana Sands (Beneatha in both the stage and film versions of *A Raisin in the Sun*) was originally cast as Claudine. Indeed she had started filming when she collapsed on set, deteriorated rapidly, and finally succumbed to cancer. Most of those involved believed Diahann to be wrong as replacement, given her image as a glamorous chanteuse of the jet set. Although Carroll was viewed as a "bronze barbie doll," Sands recognized her ability, potential, and versatility and lobbied for her to be cast as Claudine. Ironically, years earlier, Carroll had read for the part of Beneatha in *A Raisin in the Sun,* losing out to Sands. Somewhat later, it was Carroll's chance to be benefactress. Carroll pushed successfully to engage Sands for a continuing role on her series *Julia* (1968–1971), in which Carroll played the title role as a single mother. In her autobiography, Carroll comments, "without Diana's perseverance, I'm certain the film [*Claudine*] would never have happened." Sands died during filming, and Carroll never had a chance to thank her in person. At Sands's wake, Diahann recalls, "As I said goodbye, I told her how much I would miss her and promised to be the best damn Claudine possible—the best ever!"

Claudine was an outgrowth of the Third World Cinema Corporation, which was organized to produce (in New York City) films utilizing the talents of blacks, Puerto Ricans, and other minority groups and to distribute them to motion picture houses and television networks. Third World trained many of the directors and technicians who have been working on films produced by black filmmakers since the 1980s.

In *Claudine*, Carroll plays a Harlem domestic worker who must cope with a desperate situation. She falls in love with a sanitation worker played effectively by James Earl Jones. Claudine is a single mom raising six children while working and receiving supplementary public assistance. The film takes a refreshingly realistic look at life as it is lived by many women whose main goal is to keep their families together in spite of enormous odds. The characters are funny but never buffoons. Drawing upon her early years in Harlem, Diahann made the part of Claudine her very own. Deemed too chic by some to be a welfare mother, she had her hair pushed back severely and wore a dress that suggested "knock knees." Diahann admitted, "I have been searching desperately for a role in a film that was not a sophisticated, well-dressed, educated lady, which has been my image."

Actor/comedian Keenan Ivory Wayans saw *Claudine* as, "very close to our own personal experience in terms of having a big family and the stress of trying to keep your family together and the love within the family despite all the problems. That was the thing that had a personal effect on me when I was watching it."

Carroll claims she didn't expect to win the Oscar and as it happened she didn't. The statuette went to Ellen Burstyn for *Alice Doesn't Live Here Anymore*. However Diahann feels that the honor of an Academy Award nomination for *Claudine* was and remains thrilling. A personal benefit from the nomination was meeting her third husband, Robert De Leon, then managing editor of *Jet*. He met the star covering her Academy nomination story for his magazine. As they say, the rest was history.

1981

Howard E. Rollins Jr.

b. October 17, 1950, Baltimore, Maryland
d. December 8, 1996, New York, New York

Nominee, Best Supporting Actor, 1981
COALHOUSE WALKER in *Ragtime*

Howard Rollins had no formal training as an actor. Since he was virtually unknown, he doubted director Milos Forman would cast him in *Ragtime*. Arriving for his second screen test and seeing O. J. Simpson emerging, he thought it was all over. In addition, other big-name performers, such as Louis Gossett Jr. and Richard Pryor, were said to have been interested in the role of Coalhouse Walker. When Howard learned he had landed the film role, he fell to his knees and started to weep.

The film is based on the E. L. Doctorow novel *Ragtime,* and the character Coalhouse is a fiery turn-of-the-century piano player turned revolutionary, insisting on justice. Coalhouse seeks redress for his grievance after his automobile is deliberately wrecked by white racists. As protest, he takes over the J. P. Morgan Library in New York City and threatens to blow it up. In a scene in which Coalhouse plays the organ at his wife's funeral, tears stream readily down Rollins's face. The actor wasn't merely acting; he had become Coalhouse. Said Rollins, "I'd like Coalhouse to be seen not just as a terrorist but as a man of principle and action. He has exhausted every legal means at his disposal and is left with no other choice."

Rollins had been compared to Sidney Poitier countless times, and it made some sense in that Poitier was an early inspiration for Rollins, who admitted, "with the exception of Sidney Poitier there were hardly any precedents I could look at and say, I'll be like that."

Understandingly, Rollins added, "I'm not the new Sidney Poitier, I'm the first Howard Rollins."

Despite what a critic described as a volcanic performance as Coalhouse Walker, stealing the spotlight from veteran star James Cagney, Rollins's nomination for a screen debut performance did not produce an Oscar. The trophy went instead to the distinguished British thespian Sir John Gielgud for *Arthur*. As is the case more often than not, Howard's nomination did little to advance his career. He had to wait four years for another acceptable film role to come along— Captain Davenport in *A Soldier's Story*. Howard's father died without seeing that film, but the Bethlehem steel worker, never inside a movie theater before, did see *Ragtime* five times with unabashed parental pride.

Fame exacted its toll, and for a long period of time Rollins struggled with substance abuse problems. His untimely death came at age forty-six in 1996. As an extraneous epilogue, seventeen years after the film, *Ragtime* went on to become a highly successful award-winning musical on Broadway.

1982

Louis Gossett Jr.

b. May 27, 1936, Brooklyn, New York

Winner, Best Supporting Actor, 1982
SERGEANT EMIL FOWLEY in *An Officer and a Gentleman*

There was a notion before *An Officer and a Gentleman* was made that no one could really make anything out of what appeared on paper as a colorless role. Gossett's part was originally intended for a Caucasian actor, which explains its race-neutral nature in the completed film. Gossett's agent kept calling the studio and finally confronted the director, asking why the sergeant couldn't be black. Taylor Hackford, the director, met with Gossett, and the role became his. Up until that point, Hackford had seen no actor who fit the part.

To prepare himself for the role, Gossett spent ten days in a drill instructors training school at Camp Pendleton, California. The plot features Gossett as a relentless, hard-as-nails, ramrod-straight drill instructor. He puts the lead character, played by Richard Gere, through grueling training, turning him ultimately into a true navy man. *Newsweek* wrote, "Gossett's whiplike edge manages to make a hackneyed character seem almost fresh."

The Oscar nomination for Sergeant Fowley was somewhat unexpected, given that this character exhibits no personal life outside of his relationship to Gere's character. For his performance Gossett won a Golden Globe and an NAACP Image Award, as well as the coveted Oscar. In the period following his Oscar win, Lou experienced the worst depression of his life. "I expected a lot more to happen—I mean the first black since Sidney Poitier to win an Oscar. Well, nothing happened. I let myself become bitter, resentful. I was my own worst enemy. I said to myself, 'what more can I do? where's the light at the end of the tunnel?' I started to self-destruct." All these feelings led to substance abuse. Lou's subsequent recovery was aided by his participation in a residential treatment program.

In 1982, it had been nearly two decades since an African American had won an Oscar for acting, which might have given Gossett a slight edge. At a pre-Oscar ceremony reception, Sidney Poitier, who had won in 1963, predicted, "It will be inconceivable if he [Gossett] doesn't win." Happily he did. An emotionally charged Gossett accepted the award with refreshing humility and a homage to his competitors, "And all you other four guys, THIS IS OURS."

1983

Alfre Woodard

b. *November 8, 1952, Tulsa, Oklahoma*

Nominee, Best Supporting Actress, 1983
GEECHEE in *Cross Creek*

Alfre Woodard has never made a film of which she need be ashamed (no exploitation, no gratuitous sex). With one of the most expressive faces in cinema, she communicates strength and humanity in every role. Alfre's unique name came from a vision in which, her godmother insists, it was spelled out in gold letters on a wall. Speaking of letters, Alfre holds an M.A. from Boston University. Recalling Alfre's audition for *Cross Creek,* star Mary Steenburgen said, "Alfre just blew us away." On being notified in 1982 that she had been selected for the role of Geechee, an uneducated black woman who becomes friend as well as servant, Alfre remembers leaving her apartment and jumping for joy into the Pacific Ocean. She appreciated the part because it included scenes long enough to permit various shifts of emotion, every actor's dream.

Based on the memoirs of author Marjorie Kinnan Rawlings, the film's focus is on Rawlings's "coming of age" during the 1920s in the Florida swamplands. Woodard has a powerfully affirming feminist line, directed to Steenburgen as Rawlings: "I see you're a woman and you live by yourself and nobody takes advantage of you." The producer and director of *Cross Creek* had worked previously on *Sounder*, which garnered acting nominations for two African Americans, Cicely Tyson and Paul Winfield.

Although *Cross Creek* was panned by critics, Woodard's notices were all highly positive. Peter Rainer in the *Los Angeles Herald Ex-*

aminer proclaimed, "Alfre Woodard's Geechee is a small acting gem with one of the best acted monologues in movies." Arthur Knight of the *Hollywood Reporter* claimed, "Alfre Woodard builds a performance that finally tears at your heart." The *Washington Post* hailed Woodard as "an actress able to make the smallest role significant, able to inject dignity into the most banal film."

Universal Pictures, the distributors, gave little help with financing the advertising and publicity so essential to the capture of Academy attention. If Academy members don't see a film, a win or even a nomination is highly improbable. Producer Robert Radnitz resorted to distributing handbills to Academy members at a theater in Malibu where he had booked the film. Alfre Woodard gained the nomination but lost the Oscar to Linda Hunt for *The Year of Living Dangerously.*

Early in the new millennium, the acclaimed black writer Maya Angelou, while paying tribute to various individuals and their contributions to the last century, stated, "I am inspired by the excellent work of Alfre Woodard."

1984

Adolph Caesar

b. December 5, 1933, New York, New York
d. March 6, 1986, Los Angeles, California

Nominee, Best Supporting Actor, 1984
SERGEANT VERNON WATERS in *A Soldier's Story*

Adapted from Charles Fuller's Pulitzer Prize–winning play, *A Soldier's Story* is about an army officer's investigation of a murder on a Southern base. The film proved that a work that allows blacks to tell their own story can be a financial success. First-year grosses were estimated at $30 million, placing it among the studio's top earners for the year. Caesar played an alcoholic, abusive, "cussing" sergeant. His real-life stint in the navy under white officers provided him with a useful background for playing a military part. Until this film, voice-overs for commercials had kept Caesar going. Who can forget that deep bass voice saying "A mind is a terrible thing to waste" on behalf of the United Negro College Fund? Although an inexperienced film actor, Caesar possessed an abundance of self-assurance, often expressed by a click of his teeth and a wink of his eye. The actor exuded self-confidence from day one. A filmmaker who interviewed numerous persons for a job in the late 1970s recalls Caesar as the only actor who left saying "call me when you make up your mind."

Newsweek printed, "His portrait of a tragically twisted spirit is exact, uncompromising and indelible." Following the film's success, Caesar admitted, "Never in my wildest dreams could I have anticipated the reception for this film. It hasn't changed me; I refuse to let it but it has changed my status. I'm an entity, a name." The then fifty-one-year-old actor couldn't wait to do more film work. Caesar received wide recognition for the role of Sergeant Waters. He had already won OBIE and Drama Desk Awards for his work in the stage play on which the film was based when he received an NAACP Image Award for the film. However, his Academy Award nomination did not end in a victory. The Oscar for best supporting actor went to a nonprofessional actor, Haing S. Ngor, for *The Killing Fields*.

Adolph Caesar succumbed to a fatal heart attack in 1986 after only one day's shooting on *Tough Guys*, costarring Kirk Douglas and Burt Lancaster. *A Soldier's Story*'s writer, Charles Fuller, eulogized, "When a man of great talent in our history dies, we are bound not merely to denote his passing, but lament the loss for us. This is a tragic day for American theater, but a catastrophic day for the black community." Broadway's Negro Ensemble Company established the Adolph Caesar Performing Arts Award in remembrance of the late actor.

1985

Margaret Avery

b. Mangum, Oklahoma

Nominee, Best Supporting Actress, 1985
SHUG AVERY in *The Color Purple*

At first Tina Turner was mentioned for the role of Shug, the sensuous singer in *The Color Purple*. When Turner opted out, Steven Spielberg selected Avery, whom he had directed previously in a commercial. Always slim, Avery changed her diet to gain approximately twenty pounds for the part. However, she was never quite able to master the knack of inhaling for the cigarette-smoking scene. Revealing her humility, Avery confides, "When I learned what an incredible amount of talent they were seeking, I got down on my knees and prayed, 'Give me the confidence to go on!'" The role centered on a universal theme, a daughter's need for her father's approval and affection. In Shug's case her father's denial of her leads to her quest for admiration wherever she can find it. Avery's portrayal of Shug Avery (the character had the same last name as the actress) was painted using a broad pallet of humor, dramatic depth, and musicality. Although the actress sings and has enjoyed a modest career doing so, her songs were dubbed by singer Tata Vega. Turning in a radiant and strong performance, the quality of Margaret Avery's acting was beyond reproach. She expressed the wish, "that people will be so drawn into the story that they will see beyond the color of the people in it, and just see the purple."

An extraordinarily controversial advertisement in the form of a letter written in Black English became Avery's own personal bid for an Oscar. The letter read: "Dear God, I knows dat I been blessed by

Alice Walker, Steven Spielberg and Quincy Jones. Now I is up for the nomination fo' best supporting actress alongst with some fine talented ladies that I is proud to be in the company of. Your little daughter, Margaret Avery." Avery was criticized by some for the "Ebonics" style. Because three African American actresses (Whoopi, Oprah, and Avery) were nominated for their work in a single film, it was not unexpected that the NAACP denounced the Academy for not awarding the film even one Oscar despite its eleven nominations. It should be remembered that the studio only spent $100,000 on trade paper advertisements, comparatively little for a major studio. Anjelica Huston won the Oscar for *Prizzi's Honor,* directed by her famed father, John Huston.

Manifesting once again the "best supporting actress nominee curse," Margaret Avery has not been cast since in a role comparable to Shug in *The Color Purple.*

1985

Whoopi Goldberg

b. *November 13, 1949, New York, New York*

Nominee, Best Actress, 1985
CELIE in *The Color Purple*

It is alleged that Whoopi Golberg emerged at birth seeking out the light (incontrovertible proof of star quality). As an adult she demonstrated a certain versatility working as a bricklayer on a construction site at the San Diego Zoo, breaking gender barriers even then. Later she became a cosmetician in a funeral home, preparing corpses for viewing. "The customers rarely talked back," she quipped. Whoopi wrote Alice Walker asking to be in a possible film of her novel *The Color Purple*, originally eyeing the part of Sofia. Time and place can mean everything, as it did in Goldberg's casting. Steven Spielberg observed her at a party doing a hilarious spoof of *E.T.*, his film. She had E.T. landing in Oakland, strung out on drugs and winding up in the "slammer." Spielberg loved it and informed Goldberg that he was preparing a production of *The Color Purple* and would be interested in her for the role of Celie.

Film critic Roger Ebert refers to Goldberg's Celie as "one of the most amazing debut performances in movie history." Conflicting views surrounded the film. One critic made the flippant remark that he was watching the first Disney movie about incest. At the time Spielberg was seen as an unlikely director for the film's subject matter. Negative reviews were only slightly eased by compliments for its costumes and cinematography. The then head of the NAACP's Los Angeles chapter saw the film as stereotypical racism, but he lauded the fabulous acting. *The Color Purple* failed to acquire a single award from the Academy, which some attributed to its being a predominantly black film. A then inexperienced film actress, Whoopi was destined to lose the top acting Oscar to veteran actress Geraldine Page for *The Trip to Bountiful*. Page was a sentimental "her-time-has-come" favorite, having received seven previous nominations in 1953, 1961, 1962, 1966, 1972, 1978, and 1984. *The Color Purple* won five NAACP Image Awards, and Whoopi won a Golden Globe Award. The best was yet to come for the talented actress, who claimed modestly, "I am not a symbol. Anyone can do what I have done."

In the years immediately following her nomination, Whoopi earned a reputation as one of Hollywood's busiest film actresses. She has experienced her share of box office failures (*Fatal Beauty, Jumpin' Jack Flash*) as well as hits (*Sister Act, The Lion King*). Becoming somewhat "gun shy" about accepting leading roles, Goldberg stated, "I don't want to carry any more movies. I want to be good in small parts." This statement could be attributed to clairvoyance, since she took home an Oscar five years later for a small but pivotal role in *Ghost*.

1985

Oprah Winfrey

b. January 29, 1954, Kosciusko, Mississippi

Nominee, Best Supporting Actress, 1985
SOFIA in *The Color Purple*

One would never have guessed from Oprah Winfrey's strong performance as Sofia, a woman faced with unspeakable frustration and humiliation, that she had never faced a motion picture camera before *The Color Purple*. Like many other young African Americans, Oprah was inspired by Sidney Poitier when, at age ten, she watched him receive the Oscar on television. "I remember sitting on the linoleum floor in my mother's apartment in Milwaukee. I was in complete awe, first of all that a colored man arrived in a limousine, and then that he won," reminisces Oprah. Years later she was a Chicago talk show host, little known elsewhere. She used to distribute copies of *The Color Purple* to people she encountered around Chicago because she loved Alice Walker's book. Quincy Jones, co-producer of the film, had spotted her on "AM Chicago" while channel surfing in his Chicago hotel room and realized, "That's Sofia." Winfrey was eager for the challenge, entreating God to find her a way to get into the movie. A requirement to gain thirty pounds for the role of the plump Sofia created a real sacrifice for Oprah, who coped with dieting in her personal life. Casting agent Reuben Cannon warned her, "I hear you're at some fat farm. If you've lost a pound, you're in trouble."

Still the consummate television host, Oprah spoke lines such as "Well Miss Celie it's so good to see you," looking straight at the camera. Director Spielberg had to remind her that in acting you look at the other character. He admits that he wanted Oprah's terror at doing a first film to work for her in the part. Consequently he did not offer her praise and reassurance during filming. Painfully self-conscious of her lack of experience, Oprah initially thought Spielberg might fire her. Often his approach was to depend on her instinctive reactions to a situation. For one scene, he did not alert Oprah that a group of whites would be shouting "nigger" at her. Oprah gave him the performance he wanted.

During the course of the film, Sofia is transformed from a gutsy outspoken young bride to a physically and emotionally shattered older woman who is tyrannized by her racist white employers. The plot calls for Sofia's one act of defiance and self-assertion to unleash tragic consequences upon her. A number of criticisms accompanied the film's release, including the equation of Sofia with the Aunt Jemima stereotype.

On learning of her Oscar nomination, Winfrey recalls, "I always knew I'd be an actress since I was growing up on the farm in Mississippi, sitting in the pig pen talking to those pigs." Reflecting years later on film critic Gene Siskel's candor, Oprah said, Gene told her, "You are not going to win." A rhetorical question for which there can never be an acceptable answer is "How could Oprah and Whoopi Goldberg make nominee-worthy debuts under Spielberg's direction and neither one win an Oscar?"

Adding to the excitement of attending an Oscar ceremony at which she was a nominee was the apocryphal account of her gown not fitting due to unexpected weight gain. It is said that she had to lie flat on the floor to have the garment squeezed on her. The tale describes Oprah's anxiety that once she was at the auditorium the custom-fashioned gown would rip. This is a exceptional instance in which not hearing one's name called following "the envelope please" might have been a blessing.

A decade later Oprah Winfrey, black and female, had become one of the wealthiest and most powerful names in the entertainment world.

1986

Dexter Gordon

b. February 27, 1923, Los Angeles, California
d. April 25, 1990, Philadelphia, Pennsylvania

Nominee, Best Actor, 1986
DALE TURNER in 'Round Midnight

The release of Bertrand Tavernier's 'Round Midnight surprised very few movie fans, since French filmmakers have traditionally explored the use of modern jazz in their films. The plot concerns a burned-out jazz musician who is persuaded by a devoted French fan to forsake alcohol and drugs in order to try for a comeback in New York. This effort succeeds for a brief time, but ultimately the musician reverts to his own self-destruction. Those who might dismiss the film as just another black male/white male buddy construct of the 1980s should be reminded that the script was based on the real-life relationship between legendary jazz musician Bud Powell and Francis Paudras, a young French designer who befriended him in Europe. The film was dedicated to the memory of Powell and Lester Young.

Dexter Gordon had a somewhat checkered past. In the 1940s, he played saxophone with the Lionel Hampton and Billy Eckstine bands. Drug problems deterred him from realizing his full musical potential in live performances as well as recordings. In 1954 Gordon played a bit part in Unchained, a film about Chino prison, where he was an inmate at the time for drug charges. He was seen as a musician, but his playing was dubbed by Georgie Auld. California's Chino was an experimental prison without bars.

When Dexter Gordon returned from Europe in 1976, he discovered that the audience for mainstream jazz was alive and well. That year he garnered deserved praise for a successful gig at the Village

Vanguard. Gordon had always been "tight" with fellow musicians such as Kenny Clarke and John Coltrane as well as the aforementioned Bud Powell.

Although Herbie Hancock picked up an Oscar for best original score for *'Round Midnight,* Gordon lost the best actor award to Paul Newman in *The Color of Money,* which was a righteous win, given that Newman had been nominated six times previously as best actor but had never won the prize.

For an African American jazz musician to achieve a nomination as one of the five best actors in the leading role category is an extraordinary feat. Those naysayers who disparage the accomplishment of an expatriate saxophonist playing an expatriate saxophonist surely must realize that such Hollywood legends as John Wayne and Gary Cooper virtually played themselves on the big screen and were rewarded with Oscars.

Dexter Gordon died in 1990 at age sixty-seven.

1987

Morgan Freeman

b. June 1, 1937, Memphis, Tennessee

Nominee, Best Supporting Actor, 1987
Leo "Fast Black" Smalls in *Street Smart*

Freeman admits he had no hesitation in taking the role of a violent, venomous, and psychologically manipulative pimp. He acknowledges, "Having grown up in the South, I'm very aware of my blackness, but I'm an actor first. I play roles as they appear to me not as I imagine they will appear to other people." Playing a pimp for the first time was an unquestionable challenge. Fast Black is a genial man with a vicious personality; he is older and wiser than most pimps. Freeman respects the role that physicality plays in preparing a character. He had his hair relaxed and his nails manicured and extended, since some pimps have long nails. Moreover, he added a gold cap to a front tooth that flashed when he smiled. The actor admits he had observed some pimps who lived in SRO (single-room occupancy) hotels near where he resided on the Upper West Side of Manhattan. He truly fleshed out the character and perceived the role as "an opportunity to put my own stamp on a real bad guy."

Harlem's black community took issue with *Street Smart*'s production company for having no black camera personnel at a time when black images were projected on screen as the negative three *P*s: pimps, prostitutes, and pushers.

Morgan Freeman's nomination was viewed by the "in crowd" as a long shot to win. Even before the Oscar ceremony, Sean Connery was reputed to be a shoo-in for his powerful performance in *The Untouchables*, the Al Capone drama, which was light years away from his identification as James Bond. Though Freeman did lose to Connery, this was only the first of several Academy Award nominations in store for the versatile actor.

Freeman's success as an actor appears to have been predestined from the early age of twelve, when he was a huge hit as "Little Boy Blue" in a school production. Clearly Freeman has been consistently attracted to performing, even dancing in a chorus at the 1964 World's Fair. If he ever doubted himself, vindication most surely arrived in the form of a rhetorical question proffered by the renown film critic Pauline Kael, "Is there a better American actor than Morgan Freeman?"

In 2002, Morgan Freeman had his hand- and footprints cemented into Hollywood's famed Grauman's Chinese Theatre forecourt, joining Sidney Poitier, Whoopi Goldberg, and Denzel Washington, other African American film stars who have been so honored.

1987

Denzel Washington

b. December 28, 1954, Mount Vernon, New York

Nominee, Best Supporting Actor, 1987
STEVEN BIKO in *Cry Freedom*

For the part of Steven Biko, Denzel Washington interviewed people on three continents who had known Biko. He read everything he could find about the activist, including *Biko* and *Asking for Trouble,* written by Donald Woods, a white South African editor who had been Biko's friend. While researching the role, Washington was privileged to listen to audiotapes and view rare video footage of Biko. It was natural for Denzel to be captivated by Biko's mind, because he himself is among the most analytical of actors. Denzel's goal as he saw it was truth, not propaganda. "I'm an actor; I've never chosen a role for political or social reasons; I've never said, 'This year, I'm only doing political roles'; that would be stupid." Moved by months on location in Zimbabwe, Denzel recalls, "I'll never forget Africa. I really felt the desire, the longing for my roots. . . . I felt very comfortable there." In addition to removing his teeth caps and growing a goatee, an undaunted Washington had simulated a South African accent even while surrounded by authentic South African actors. Denzel's first trip to South Africa gave him a small taste of Apartheid. During the shoot he received threats such as having his head and other vital parts of his body cut off.

The selection of Sir Richard Attenborough as director was seen by some as providing prestige for an explosive theme. Attenborough had been successful in helming the film biography of Gandhi, dealing with another minority group. Ostensibly about Steven Biko, the martyred black South African beaten to death in police custody, the film swiftly devolved into a melodrama about what inconveniences and consequences a white family must endure for befriending the black protagonist. It was not surprising then that Biko, portrayed by Denzel, dies early in the film, easing the way for *Cry Freedom* to be promoted (at least by word of mouth) as "the Kevin Kline movie." The subliminal message to white moviegoers is: "the theme may appear to be black but it is not really about them, it is about us."

Although Denzel is only in approximately one-third of the film, his performance is electrifying and superb. Denzel was disappointed that several of his speeches had been cut from the final print. "To me, the speeches were the more important part of playing the role. To be able to say those words, the very words that he [Biko] wrote and spoke, and not some version thereof—that was of such importance to me," said Washington.

Denzel was one of two African Americans to be nominated as best actor in a supporting role; the other was Morgan Freeman. Both lost to Sean Connery for *The Untouchables*. Experiencing an all-too-familiar post-Oscar nomination phenomenon, Denzel found that Hollywood film gigs were not forthcoming. The only offer was for *The Mighty Quinn*, an independent whodunit. Following that melodrama, Denzel did a brief run on Broadway in *Checkmates*, costarring Paul Winfield, 1972 Oscar nominee.

Concerning Oscar, Denzel claims he doesn't quite know how to take such awards, partly because the craft of acting is still, in many ways, mysterious to him. "Some days you're just swimming through Jello, no matter what you do. Other days you can do no wrong and people ask you to take credit for it. Who knows?" Whenever interviewers mention Oscar buzz to Denzel, he retorts, "Better than not talking about you." The actor remembers being late for his first Oscar ceremony, because his limousine got stuck in traffic. Refusing to get out and walk, he was determined to arrive in style, not suspecting that it would be the first of many successive Oscar events.

1989

Morgan Freeman

b. June 1, 1937, Memphis, Tennessee

Nominee, Best Actor, 1989
HOKE COLBURN in *Driving Miss Daisy*

The role that brought Morgan Freeman his second Academy nomination (his first in the leading role category) was accompanied by allegations of it being an Uncle Tom stereotype. Alfred Uhry, who wrote the play, knew that an intelligent "stand-up" professional like Morgan Freeman would never have even considered playing the role in an Uncle Tom vein. Recently however, Chris Rock quipped that the only advice Freeman had given him on the *Nurse Betty* set was "Don't trust whitey," a joke that played on an unwarranted view of Freeman as a nonmilitant. Some students at Emory University cringed at the actions of Hoke Colburn, aghast at the racial manners of an era predating their birth. Actually the strength of Freeman's performance was in his not giving Hoke an anachronistic post–Civil Rights Era attitude and sensibility. Freeman reflects, "Hoke was the one everybody wanted to call Uncle Tom. That man who could get through it, could do it all and smile. He had all that dignity." As bizarre as it sounds, a producer at one time mentioned the possibility of casting actor-comedian Eddie Murphy as Hoke. Only in Hollywood!

Freeman had won the Golden Globe (considered by many as a predictor of an Oscar win). The National Board of Reviewers tendered honors to Freeman for his performance as the low-keyed, patient, and dignified chauffeur. He was nominated for an Academy Award as best actor in a leading role. The part of Hoke called for underplaying, in contrast to the high-gear theatricality displayed by competitor Daniel Day-Lewis as a cerebral palsy victim in *My Left Foot*. Lewis took home the statuette.

Working against Freeman for the award was the fact that his costar Jessica Tandy won an Oscar as best actress and *Driving Miss Daisy* won as best picture of the year. Even though Tandy and Freeman were a "duet ensemble," playing off each other as a Southern Jewish widow and her black chauffeur, only five times before in Academy history had two major acting awards been bestowed on the same film: *It Happened One Night* (1934), *One Flew Over the Cuckoo's Nest* (1975), *Network* (1976), *Coming Home* (1978), and *On Golden Pond* (1981).

In the supporting actor category, Denzel Washington won an Oscar, for *Glory*, a film in which Freeman also had a supporting role. Morgan describes his acting preparation as "seat of the pants" as opposed to Denzel's studied approach. A look at Morgan's performance in the 1990 fiasco *The Bonfire of the Vanities* establishes that an Oscar is well within Morgan Freeman's grasp. Who can forget his authoritative judge, reproaching "out of control" courtroom spectators, "Decency is what your grandmother taught you." It is a memorable line uttered in Freeman's uniquely forceful manner.

1989

Spike Lee

b. March 20, 1957, Atlanta, Georgia

Nominee, Best Screenplay, 1989
Do the Right Thing

Spike Lee's motivation for making *Do the Right Thing* evolved from circumstances in his life. The summer following his graduation from film school, he served an eight-week internship at Columbia Pictures, where he saw a dearth of faces of color. He was convinced that for him to make it, the independent route would be the way. Another catalyst was the racially incited death of a young black man in Howard Beach.

Spike drew heavily on the New York talent bank in casting his film. He was of the opinion that Los Angeles actors were drawn toward becoming stars, while New York actors were more inclined to be concerned about the work. Hence his cast included Ossie Davis, Ruby Dee, Giancarlo Esposito, and Bill Nunn as Radio Rayheem. Initially Spike wanted Laurence Fishburne for that role, but Fishburne was already on the path to leading roles.

Do the Right Thing is set in the Bedford Stuyvesant area of Brooklyn. It is an explosive environment of tension and frustration borne out of poverty, racism, and police brutality. Spike wanted audiences to confront these powerful issues of life in urban America. Ernest Dickerson's brilliant cinemaphotography enhanced the vision of an extremely hot summer day on one street block in Brooklyn.

Political polarization encompassed the film, with predictions that the depiction of a Bed-Stuy neighborhood erupting into racial violence after a black youth is killed by police would evoke violence wherever it was screened. On the other hand, Lee saw the film as a reflection of society and a hard look at race relations between two ethnic groups (African Americans and Italian Americans) within a neighborhood. Some critics thought that when the character Mookie throws the trash can through the store window, it might be seen as a metaphoric invitation to widespread urban rioting. Others assailed Lee's ambivalence in his film's ending. An epilogue has one quote from Martin Luther King Jr. denouncing violence and one quote from Malcolm X espousing the "by any means necessary" credo. Former New York City Mayor Ed Koch believed the film to be contentious and filled with racial hatred directed at both whites and blacks. Not all responses to the film were negative. Reverend Al Sharpton of the National Action Network stated, "It was a turning point for how the last generation of the twentieth century would deal with social questions. It was far more than a movie." Betty Shabazz, the widow of Malcolm X, was quoted as saying, "I saw this film as, for all those people who live in ivory towers, who don't get into the inner city. It says that we need to do something. The film emphasizes our mutual humanity." Film critics Roger Ebert and Gene Siskel sang the film's praises, according it a place on their annual ten best list. Siskel pronounced, "Spike has all the ammunition of a great filmmaker and shows it." Referring to the film, Ebert said, "it dealt with the most important subject in America today and did so in a way that a viewer of any race could come away with a better understanding of what moves other groups." Budgeted at $6.5 million, the film grossed a not-too-shabby $28 million domestically, despite its controversial "ups and downs."

Spike Lee has had a long-term connection with the Academy of Motion Picture Arts and Sciences, however tenuous. Graduating from New York University's film school, he received a student Academy Award for his thesis film, "Joe's Bed-Stuy Barber Shop: We Cut Heads." *Do the Right Thing* received two Oscar nominations, the other one going to Danny Aiello as best supporting actor. It did not receive a nomination for best director or best picture. Nominated for best screenplay, Lee lost the Oscar to Tom Schulman for *Dead Poets Society*. At the ceremony, actress Kim Basinger, a presenter in another category, digressed long enough to comment on the Academy's insufficient recognition of *Do the Right Thing*. Spike has been among the most caustic critics of the Academy's Oscar choices. During a dialogue with fellow filmmaker Martin Scorsese, Spike ranted, "Best picture of the year, *Driving Miss Daisy*? After that, I said, I give up! What can you do?" Scorsese's response was, "You can't do anything about it." Addressing an audience at Whittier College, Spike blasted the Oscars as "a popularity contest voted on mostly by white males over fifty years old."

Now available on DVD, *Do the Right Thing* is considered by many as the most important work from a black filmmaker in the last twenty-five years. At the Academy's Seventy-first awards ceremony, in 1998, a rapid montage representing one hundred years of cinema included a snippet from the film.

The Library of Congress has included it in its National Film Registry, as culturally, historically, and aesthetically significant and consequently worthy of preservation.

Spike Lee summarizes his work with the comment, "I respect the audience's intelligence a lot and that's why I don't try to go for the lowest common denominator."

1989

Denzel Washington

b. December 24, 1954, Mount Vernon, New York

Winner, Best Supporting Actor, 1989
TRIPP in *Glory*

Denzel Washington never wanted the mantle of being the first black matinee idol since Sidney Poitier. Avoiding the "climbing Mount Poitier syndrome," he just wanted to be evaluated on his own merit.

Washington had been given his choice of two roles in *Glory*, a defiant orphaned slave or an educated freed man. He opted for the former, and the role he passed on went to Andre Braugher. Denzel claims he didn't know why he made the choice he did, but he was obviously delighted with the outcome. Initially he had a block about doing a slave film with beatings and all the other trappings of the genre. Denzel invested an incredible amount of effort and research in preparing for the role. His barber was instructed to give him a bald head, which afforded the physicality of a slave. Ed Zwick, the director, sees Denzel as quick and intelligent, a man whose process may not be academic but who is certainly thorough. He seems to possess some kind of profound and intense relaxation that allows him as an actor to be fully in the moment rather than needing to resort to emotional hype. Above all Denzel has an extraordinary sense of presence. Shooting the film in Georgia, the actor drew from deep within himself, realizing that by summoning up the collective spirit of former slaves, he would breathe more reality into the role.

Denzel portrays Tripp, a runaway, embittered, former slave who has joined the Fifty-fourth Massachusetts Regiment, the first black unit to fight for the Union in the Civil War. The black soldiers depicted in the film fought not only for the preservation of the Union but for their freedom from slavery. *Glory* makes a very strong antiwar statement in telling the story of this black brigade under the command of a young and naive white colonel. Denzel hoped fervently that *Glory* would not become another *Cry Freedom,* in which he appeared earlier. That story, ostensibly about a black, became transformed into a paean to white heroism.

A scene that could not fail to move audiences was the one in which Tripp is stripped to the waist, tied to a post, and beaten for being AWOL in search of much-needed food and shoes for his fellow black soldiers. A close-up reveals a silent and unwhimpering Tripp with eyes exuding resistance and a single tear rolling down his cheek. Another memorable scene takes place around a campfire. Washington recalls that it was largely improvisation, with very few scripted lines. Although *Glory* received rave notices, it did not fare well at the box office. Film critic Roger Ebert is on record with a prophetic comment about Denzel, saying that "nobody has seen his full range yet . . . romantic, funny, attractive—a star."

Denzel recognized that you can't really fight for an Oscar, but you will want to. While filming *Mo' Better Blues,* he did spend free time away from the set campaigning for and doing publicity in support of his nomination. Denzel's winning the Oscar on March 26, 1990, for a supporting role performance represented the first African American actor to win in this category since Lou Gossett Jr., seven years earlier. Denzel recalls, "I looked out at all those big stars the night I won and thought none of these guys [Tom Cruise, Sylvester Stallone, Arnold Schwarzenegger] . . . has an Academy Award and I know all of them want one." Denzel was aware of all the people who walked by before the ceremony, not talking to him; they all talked to him following his victory. As a winner Denzel mused, "The chase is always better than the capture," and jokingly he added, "The only thing better than having one is having two."

Family and race have always been important factors in the life of Denzel Washington. He remembers with warm amusement his mother's desire to take home the floral centerpiece from their table at the Academy's Governors Ball. It seemed incongruous to leave the place with a golden statuette and a floral arrangement. He was touched by his then five-year-old son wanting to make his dad an Oscar out of clay. An optimistic Denzel promised to bring the real trophy home for his boy's show-and-tell at school. Winning an Oscar for *Glory* undoubtedly gives Denzel the credibility for speaking to children about the accomplishments of black heroes.

Receiving his second NAACP Image Award, this time for *Glory*, carried special meaning for Denzel, because it denoted the recognition of his fellow African Americans.

In 1998, a $2.6 million, eleven-foot bronze statue in Washington, D.C., was dedicated to the black veterans of the Civil War. Arguably, Denzel's Oscar-winning role in *Glory* served as a catalyst for the overdue national acknowledgment of their military achievement.

1990

Whoopi Goldberg

b. November 13, 1949, New York, New York

Winner, Best Supporting Actress, 1990
ODA MAE BROWN in *Ghost*

In selecting her theatrical name, the actress whose real name was Caryn Johnson initially focused on Whoopi Coussin, French for whoopee cushion. Fortunately she must have realized the limitations such a name would impose. Despite her non-Eurocentric beauty, she appears to have no trouble getting work. Hollywood's acceptance of her unique look and indelible style remains a source of wonder. Whoopi Goldberg is perhaps the only black female performer who can switch from television to film, from drama to comedy. With an abundance of unmemorable roles in forgettable films since her debut in *The Color Purple,* Whoopi was fortunate to be cast as Oda Mae in *Ghost.* Consideration of Tina Turner for the role and a failed search for an unknown actress finally led to the casting of Whoopi.

Ghost's plot deals with the mugging death of its hero, Sam, (Patrick Swayze), who in his ghostly state tries to warn his grieving girlfriend (Demi Moore) that she is also in danger. A storefront spiritual adviser and medium (Whoopi) is the only person who can communicate with the ghost and relay his messages to his lover. About Whoopi, a *New York Times* writer stated, "She bridged the usually segregated worlds of the dead and the living with a vigor that gave the movie both comic relief and common sense."

Goldberg became the second black woman to receive an Oscar as best supporting actress, the first being Hattie McDaniel in 1939 for *Gone with the Wind.* Denzel Washington, the previous year's best supporting actor for *Glory*, presented the Oscar to Whoopi, making it the first time one black actor could pass the honor to another black actor. Goldberg confessed to being forced to forgo the four-letter words she might instinctively use to express her joy at winning, at least while she was at the Academy podium. Backstage she could relax, remove her shoes and admit that she was "f—king" thrilled. She also confides, "I know you're not supposed to be excited about it. I know you're supposed to be too hip . . . but it's great!" A spontaneous and truly moving acceptance speech imparted, "I want to thank everybody who makes movies. I come from New York where when I was a little kid I lived in the projects. You're the people I watched; you're the people who made me want to be an actor; I'm proud to be here; I'm so proud to be an actor and I'm going to keep on acting. For every kid out there, remember you can do it!" For *Ghost*, Whoopi also won a British Academy Award and a Golden Globe. Unabashedly proud of her Oscar, Goldberg has displayed it at every opportunity, whether on a beautiful table in her New York apartment, while traveling on lengthy trips away from home, or in her *Hollywood Squares* dressing room.

Continuing to make history in Hollywood, Goldberg became the first African American woman to solo host the Academy Awards ceremony in 1994, repeating her success in this capacity in 1996, 1999, and 2002. Demonstrating her uncanny ability to tweak an audience at the 1999 ceremony, she quipped, "I thought the black list was me and Hattie McDaniel."

Whoopi Goldberg has developed a reputation for taking on film roles that are not usually offered to a woman, let alone an African American. She has become a one-woman opponent of race bias and gender bias casting. The last line in *Ghost*, directed by Sam to Oda Mae, is "Your mother would be proud of you"; the line by extension could be directed to Whoopi Goldberg herself.

1991

John Singleton

b. January 6, 1968, Los Angeles, California

Nominee, Best Director and Best Screenplay, 1991
Boyz 'n the Hood

At age twenty-four, John Singleton became the youngest filmmaker (shattering Orson Welles's record) and the first African American to be nominated for an Oscar as best director.

Excited about movies from an early age, John is determined to be in the business of making films for the long haul. As a workaholic, Singleton confesses, "I treat making movies like it's a nine to five job, because it's the only job I've ever had on a permanent basis." Before entering the industry, he drove shuttle vans to and from the airport, worked as a messenger and in a department store. Reminiscing about his own early filmgoing, Singleton remembers the strong black male character Shaft and sees himself walking in the path of Gordon Parks, *Shaft*'s director. Singleton created New Deal Productions in 1989 while he was still in film school. He views filmmaking as a language, similar to French, Spanish, or the languages of computers. Staying with that metaphor, Singleton owns up to finally creating his own dialect, his own special style. He had just completed a writing course at the University of Southern California when he began *Boyz 'n the Hood* on location in South Central Los Angeles.

When Columbia Pictures became interested in his script, an inexperienced but confident Singleton insisted on being the director of his work. Most of the bad films made about black people have been directed by people who aren't African American. Singleton wasn't about to let some (however well-intended) fool from Idaho or Encino direct a movie about life in South Central L.A. If Columbia didn't want to make the movie with him directing, it didn't want to make the movie, he firmly believed. As lonely as the presence of an African American executive can be at a Hollywood studio, it can mean a great deal when it comes to the acceptance or rejection of a black film project. An African American woman production executive at Columbia at the time played an important role in getting the studio to "green light" Singleton's first film.

The movie about life on the mean streets of South Central focuses on three young men: Ricky, a high school father who hopes to attend U.S.C.; his brother Doughboy, an unemployed drug dealer on parole; and their neighbor, Tre Styles. Tre is the teenage son of divorced parents who are both determined that he follow the straight and narrow. As Tre, Cuba Gooding Jr. goes through an emotional gamut when his friend is slain on the street. Gooding received rave reviews for his performance. The role of Furious Styles, Tre's father, was inspired by Singleton's own father. Furious guides, nurtures, and teaches his son how to be a strong black man. Lawrence Fishburne played the part, and Singleton claims that he learned from Fishburne that the best acting is no acting at all. Singleton wrote the character Doughboy especially for Ice Cube, feeling that his music reflected the unique experience depicted in the film. The crew of *Boyz 'n the Hood* was 90 percent black, a remarkable accomplishment in and of itself.

A billboard proclaimed, "John Singleton wanted to tell the truth. Columbia Pictures gave him the chance to do it." Costing a mere $6 million to produce, the film made over $57 million domestically and over $100 million worldwide. For Singleton the film had both an upside and a downside. Although the breakthrough movie carried a strong theme of antiviolence, there were incidents of gun shooting and chaos in some theaters where the film was screened. Singleton explained that the violence was not because of the film but a reflection of the urban American existence. The young director is credited with the 1990s phenomenon known as "the Singleton thing"—the rash of small independents made by black filmmakers on black themes using a preponderance of black technical staff, such as *Menace II Society* and *Straight Out of Brooklyn*. Regretfully, some of these 1990s films were ghetto shoot-em-ups with assorted hip-hop gang types. A small minority saw *Boyz 'n the Hood* as just a bunch of "niggers" killing each other, but an intelligent perception of the film was that it managed to address the issue of gang violence and the universal problem of family breakdown.

Spike Lee offered Singleton some cynical but perhaps realistic advice: "the same critics and people who championed you are gonna be after your ass. Why? Human nature! When someone new and talented arrives on the scene, it's time for all to rejoice. The first time out, everyone is your friend. The second time out, forget about it." Director Steven Spielberg praised Singleton's debut film, citing as his personal favorite the climactic scene in which Doughboy carries his brother's dead body home to their mother. Critic Roger Ebert viewed the film as "not simply a brilliant directorial debut, but an American film of enormous relevance."

Directors are nominated for Oscar by members of the Academy's Directors Branch. Bruce Davis, executive director of the Academy, saw Singleton's nomination as affirmation of the Directors Branch's liberal attitude. Barbra Streisand might not agree. Although she attained a best director nod from the Directors Guild of America for *The Prince of Tides*, the Academy's Directors Branch bypassed her in favor of Singleton, who lost the Oscar to Jonathan Demme for the acclaimed *The Silence of the Lambs*. Singleton lost the Oscar for best screenplay written directly for the screen to Callie Khouri for *Thelma and Louise*.

With his ever irreverent sense of humor, Billy Crystal, as host of the Oscar ceremony, referred to *Boyz 'n the Hood* as *The David Duke Story*, a barbed comment about traditional Ku Klux Klan headgear. Singleton believes, "The less I get mired in that Hollywood machine, the better my films will be." He adheres to advice from Oscar winner Sidney Poitier, which is "never make a film your father wouldn't admire."

Singleton's *Baby Boy*, released in 2001 shares an unmistakable connection to *Boyz 'n the Hood* in terms of theme and setting.

1992

Jaye Davidson

b. 1968, Riverside, California

Nominee, Best Supporting Actor, 1992
Dil in *The Crying Game*

As the child of a black Ghanaian father and a white English mother, Jaye was raised in the white middle-class surroundings of Hertfordshire. He once actually worked as a hairdresser and also as an assistant to the fashion designers who made Princess Diana's wedding gown. Closest to acting was his job for Disney dressed as Pluto and visiting sick children in hospitals. A casting agent saw him at a wrap party in 1990 and urged him to audition for the role in *The Crying Game*. As they say, the rest is history.

The Crying Game's Dil is a hairdresser and club singer in London. The character happens to be a transvestite in love with a British soldier who has been kidnapped by IRA terrorists. In what has been termed a brilliantly deceptive performance, Davidson attracted attention for playing a babe who is actually a boy. The film, which came in under $5 million, became a huge box office moneymaker, grossing over $63 million in the United States. One can only wonder how the film would have fared had it been released as *Oh No! My Girlfriend Has a Penis!* its Cantonese title in Hong Kong. Miramax shrewdly steered this small movie on the road to the Oscars with its marketing hype of "Don't reveal the surprise ending!" referring to Dil being a he, not a she.

Assessing his Academy nomination, Davidson modestly exclaims, "Very funny . . . it's not because I'm good, it's because it was an interesting role. It was the role that was nominated, not me."

Davidson was certainly not the first actor to receive Academy recognition while appearing in "drag" on screen. Dustin Hoffman was nominated in 1982 for playing the title role of the cross-dresser in *Tootsie*. Forest Whitaker as the kidnapped soldier in *The Crying Game* was widely praised for his work, but he was not nominated for an Oscar. The silliest form of speculation centered on how the gender-bending Davidson would appear at the Oscar ceremony, as a male or female. The Oscar went to Gene Hackman, an experienced and popular actor, for *The Unforgiven*. Since Jaye's pay was not much for the film, he admits to going back on public assistance briefly before its release. Following the Oscar nomination, Davidson played an Egyptian-style ruler in *Stargate,* or, as it has been jested, he went from drag queen to king.

In spite of his meteoric success, Jaye doubts that he will continue acting. As for his current film activity, he seems to have all but disappeared.

Selznick International Studbos,
Culver City, Calif.
September 20, 1940.

Dear Mr

Please pardon my delay in complying with
your request. Enclosed you will find the
autograph. For several months I was away on
a personal appearance tour and there was no
time to take care of the many letters that
came to me.
I also want to take this time to thank you
for your words of congratualtion on my winning
the academy award.

Sincerely yours,

Hattie McDaniel.

Hattie McDaniel.

HMcD/g

Letter responding to autograph request indicates McDaniel's humility and appreciation of her Academy Award. Courtesy of the author

Hattie McDaniel is presented her Oscar by the previous year's winner in the same category, actress Fay Bainter. Copyright © Academy of Motion Picture Arts and Sciences

James Baskett accepts special Oscar from actors Jean Hersholt and Ingrid Bergman. Copyright © Academy of Motion Picture Arts and Sciences

Sidney Poitier holds the coveted Oscar for best performance by a male in a leading role, presented by actress Anne Bancroft. Copyright © Academy of Motion Picture Arts and Sciences

A triumphant Louis Gossett Jr. holds aloft his Oscar for best performance in a supporting role. Copyright © Academy of Motion Picture Arts and Sciences

*Actress Whoopi Goldberg smiles while clutching her Oscar for best perform-
ance in a supporting role.* Copyright © Academy of Motion Picture Arts and Sciences

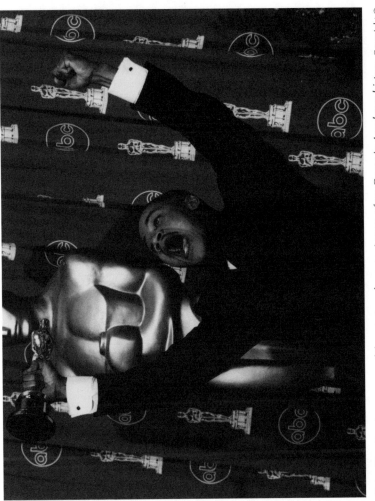

Cuba Gooding Jr. was one of the most exuberant winners of an Oscar in Academy history. Copyright © Academy of Motion Picture Arts and Sciences

Halle Berry and Denzel Washington share their joy as Academy Award winners in leading roles. Copyright © Academy of Motion Picture Arts and Sciences

1992

Denzel Washington

b. December 28, 1954, Mount Vernon, New York

Nominee, Best Actor, 1992
MALCOLM X in *Malcolm X*

This was the second time Denzel Washington had played an individual who was no longer living, Steven Biko in *Cry Freedom* having been the first. This circumstance denied the actor the privilege of consulting the source personally. Denzel had portrayed Malcolm on stage in *When the Chickens Come Home to Roost*. Washington drew on his remembrance of his own father's rhetoric as a minister who forbade his children to go to movies unless there was a biblical theme, such as in *The Ten Commandments*. For preparation Denzel interviewed Malcolm's brother and his widow, Betty Shabazz, among others, in addition to training with the Nation of Islam. "The key for me was spirit," he observes. "I am not Malcolm X, I'm Denzel but I know that the same spirit, the same God that moved him can move through me." Washington definitely did not wish either to caricature Malcolm or to soften and dilute his message. When viewing the film, people who knew the real Malcolm wondered at times if they were watching a documentary, Denzel was so convincing. He enjoyed doing the film so much that he didn't want filming to end.

Malcolm X has the distinction of being the first African American film to reach the elusive $100 million mark at the box office. Denzel had now reached a plateau of more than $10 million per movie. *Malcolm X* was based on Alex Haley's book *The Autobiography of Malcolm X*, published after the leader's assassination. Spike Lee personally distributed complimentary copies of the book to audiences attending the first-day screening in New York City.

Scripts and treatments for a film about Malcolm X had circulated around Hollywood for some years, including one by James Baldwin. Billy Dee Williams was among the actors eager to play the controversial black leader. Spike Lee was always of the opinion that only a black man should direct such a movie. For him the bottom line was about absolute control. Referring to Steven Spielberg's earlier foray into black films, Spike swore, "I'm not having no *Color Purple* fiasco on my conscience." Battling studio executives over the lengthy running time, Lee cited the more than three-hour-long Oliver Stone film *JFK*, feeling that it would be an injustice to Malcolm's life to take any shortcuts. During the editing phase, Spike discovered that he was $5 million over budget, and Warner Brothers would not bail him out. Had a Caucasian filmmaker been involved even with a marginal product, Lee believed, the studio and the bonding company would have come up with the cash. Lee was deeply moved by the generosity of a few affluent African American celebrities, such as Bill Cosby, Magic Johnson, Oprah Winfrey, and Michael Jordan, who provided funds to keep the movie afloat.

Although the film was trounced by various members of the mainstream press, as well as some of the black intelligentsia, there were good critical notices as well. The *Los Angeles Times* wrote, "Washington's Malcolm is a heroic performance in several senses, calling for him to be on screen in almost every scene and to make all those transformations believable, and the actor does it all with a special grace." Vincent Canby of the *New York Times* found, "The real triumph of *Malcolm X* is that Mr. Lee was able to make it at all. As photographed by Ernest Dickerson . . . the movie looks as authentic as any David Lean epic." Columnist Liz Smith described *Malcolm X* as a stunning feat of moviemaking. She predicted, "Spike Lee will be crying racism and ostracism again. And to tell the truth this year, he may have a point."

An Oscar win for Denzel over Al Pacino in *Scent of a Woman* was unlikely, given Pacino's four previous unsuccessful nominations—for *Serpico* in 1973, *Godfather Part II* in 1974, *And Justice for All* in 1979, and for a supporting role in *Dick Tracy* in 1990. Denzel admits, "I wanted to win. At the same time, I must say honestly, I didn't want to see Al Pacino lose. He was long overdue. . . . I'll be back." Theories abound as to why Spike Lee wasn't even nominated. A facile theory for the film's negligible recognition by the Academy's membership is racism. Was the movie evaluated on its merits or on the merits of a black effort? Another theory is retribution, because Spike is seen by some as being too arrogant, militant, and unamenable to compromise. Ruth Carter, costume designer, received the only other nomination for the film. She declares, "We felt it was a success while we were doing it. We knew it was, for us, the best picture, best cinematography, best design, best music . . . we're not concerned whether the Academy likes us or not. Spike Lee, he's the coach, and if he gives us the nod of approval, you've won." Denzel did win an NAACP Image Award and the Silver Bear at the Berlin International Film Festival for *Malcolm X*. He rightly believes that the range of roles he has played in films is helping to make Hollywood color-blind.

In 1995, Denzel Washington offered this valid point of view: "We need to concentrate on making the best films we can and not concern ourselves with who's giving us an award for it; . . . raising the standard of the work, not complaining about somebody not voting for me."

1993

Angela Bassett

b. August 16, 1958, New York, New York

Nominee, Best Actress, 1993
TINA TURNER in *What's Love Got to Do with It?*

Sitting across a table from her at the Governor's Ball following the 1997 Oscar ceremony, this author became keenly aware of the charisma and magnetic presence of Angela Bassett, which defines in part her tremendous appeal as a star. In speaking of Bassett, costar Laurence Fishburne says, "She's one of the great actresses to come along in the last twenty-five years. She's responsible for 50 percent of my performance in the film."

In the late 1980s, Angela went unsummoned to Hollywood to pursue a career in film. She was determined not to wait for the call. Bassett admits to being inspired at an early age by artists like Sidney Poitier, Dorothy Dandridge, and Cicely Tyson. She had seen James Earl Jones act on stage in *Of Mice and Men*. Angela may have been destined to play Tina Turner. She had auditioned for a part in a television series, which she didn't get. Had she succeeded, Angela would not have been available to play the self-punishing, finally liberated Tina.

Useful to Bassett in making the film was her own recollection of physical abuse inflicted on women she knew by their boyfriends. She had thirty days to work out and diet in an effort to approximate Tina's buff physique. Angela had read and reread the script, which was based on Turner's autobiography *I, Tina*. Tina Turner helped Angela perfect the unique Turner dance style and movements. She also offered guidance with the wigs, the makeup, the dresses—indeed full support. Bassett clarifies, "We're two Southern girls. Tina's a black woman from the South and so am I." Her voice was dubbed for the singing sequences with Tina's recordings. The "Proud Mary" number took two 17-hour days of shooting. Bassett claims, "Tina was the most difficult role I've ever done physically, emotionally, spiritually. It was seventeen hours every day, either performing on stage in high heels or getting beaten up."

Angela's ability to "transform herself memorably into the kind of hard-working powerhouse Ms. Turner is on stage" was commented on by Janet Maslin in the *New York Times*. The *Wall Street Journal* wrote, "Ms Bassett is simply amazing. She has somehow found the passage to Ms. Turner's spirit, to her uniquely poignant eroticism."

Angela Bassett and Laurence Fishburne became the first black actress and black actor to be nominated by the Academy for leading roles in the same film since Cicely Tyson and Paul Winfield in *Sounder* (1972). Bassett lost the Oscar to actress Holly Hunter in *The Piano*, but she did receive a Golden Globe for her performance.

1993

Laurence Fishburne

b. July 30, 1961, Augusta, Georgia

Nominee, Best Actor, 1993
IKE TURNER in *What's Love Got to Do with It?*

Finding the role of Ike Turner too demonic and having no desire to push the "evil black male" envelope, Fishburne rejected overtures more than once. He accepted the part when he learned that Angela Bassett, with whom he had worked in *Boyz 'n the Hood,* had been signed to play Tina Turner. The Ike role was not well balanced, since the script was written clearly from the perspective of Tina. Playing Ike was really scary for Fishburne because of the violence perpetrated on Tina. When the real Ike appeared on set, Fishburne enlisted his help with the "Ike walk" and informed him that he would try to make the character more human, which does not equate to sympathetic. Changing the film characterization of Ike from pure devil in the script has been attributed partially to Fishburne's rewriting suggestions. A proven playwright, Fishburne fervently desired to avoid stereotyping. Although he looked nothing like Ike physically, the actor managed to capture the essence of Ike's conflicted and tormented personality. Before Fishburne as Ike gets violent in the film, he imbues the character with a raw sex appeal.

The critics loved his work. Janet Maslin of the *New York Times* praised his performance as "brilliant, mercurial." Terrence Rafferty of the *New Yorker* commented, "The actor builds in precise increments, a devastating portrait of a macho control freak, and the amazing thing about the performance is that Fishburne finds a ghastly human in the character's madness." John Leonard is among those who believed Fishburne should have won an Oscar for his performance, but explains "that we all hated Ike for beating up on Tina." The Oscar went to Tom Hanks for *Philadelphia*.

Amidst the kudos directed toward him, Fishburne's own praise has been reserved for Sidney Poitier, an African American film star for half a century. Fishburne confesses, "I wanted to be this man."

1994

Morgan Freeman

b. June 1, 1937, Memphis, Tennessee

Nominee, Best Actor, 1994
ELLIS BOYD "RED" REDDING in *The Shawshank Redemption*

Playing a worldly-wise inmate, Morgan Freeman received his third Oscar nod for *The Shawshank Redemption*, which earned a total of seven nominations, including one for best picture. Based on popular writer Stephen King's story "Rita Hayworth and the Shawshank Redemption," the film was lensed on location in Mansfield, Ohio. Freeman recalls a considerable amount of on-set tension among the actors, producers, and the director.

Freeman portrays a hardened but humane life-sentenced prisoner who befriends a mild-mannered new inmate at Shawshank State Prison. The younger prisoner, Andy, played by Tim Robbins, killed his unfaithful wife and her lover. Freeman's character, Redding, shows Andy the ropes and what he needs to survive incarceration, all the while displaying a sly wit and inner strength. Around the prison, Redding is known as "Mr. Procure It" because he is able to acquire anything from a chisel to a Rita Hayworth poster. The plot underscores the close symbiotic relationship between the two men. When Andy escapes, Redding verbalizes a goal unlikely of fulfillment: "I hope to see my friend and shake his hand . . . I hope the Pacific is as blue as it has been in my dreams."

In 1996, an *Entertainment Weekly* survey revealed that Freeman was an extremely underpaid film actor. He received only $6 million per flick while starring in such box office hits as *Seven* and *Unforgiven*. Other male stars with box office duds were getting $15 to $20 million per picture. One could say that Freeman's lack of remuneration was certainly offset by an abundance of professional admiration and respect. Brilliant young actor Andre Braugher credits Freeman, along with Denzel Washington, for counseling him on the set of his first film, *Glory*. When the two seasoned actors appeared, "I didn't know how to act in front of a camera, and I would've fallen on my face without them telling me how," admits Braugher. The other African American Academy Award nominee in 1994, Samuel L. Jackson, claimed that Freeman for years had been a role model and a source of inspiration.

Moving into the area of digital technology, Morgan Freeman currently has his own production company, but still manages to be among the most prolific film actors.

1994

Samuel L. Jackson

b. December 21, 1948, Washington, D.C.

Nominee, Best Supporting Actor, 1994
JULES WINNFIELD in *Pulp Fiction*

Who is Samuel L. Jackson? The "L" stands for Leroy, a source of some childhood angst, with neighborhood kids chanting, "Hey Leroy, your mama's calling you." An only child, Sam was comfortable being alone with his own thoughts. A movie fan, he was drawn to the excitement and drama of *Treasure Island*, a film of Robert Louis Stevenson's classic, with its hooks and eye patches. Always into drama, even as a boy, he used ketchup and sanitary napkins to play wounded heroes. Errol Flynn movies attracted him because of their action. In those days, Sam lived under the segregated laws of life in Chattanooga, Tennessee. While he was a student at Morehouse in the 1960s, a speech professor offered extra credit to students who would act in a school production. This was a propitious opportunity for Sam, a stutterer since childhood. Sam later lived for many years in New York City, working as a stage actor, married to actress LaTanya Richardson. He readily admits, "I was a successful drug user for twenty-something years until I started smoking crack cocaine. It doesn't take long to come to your knees when that happens." When he played the crackhead Gator in Spike Lee's *Jungle Fever*, he knew the character well. For this role, Sam received a supporting actor award created especially for him at the Cannes Film Festival. Jackson is candid on the subject of Spike Lee. Slated to do a role in *Malcolm X*, Sam refused to audition for the part or to work for scale. Samuel Jackson believed he had, based on past performance, already proven himself to Spike.

When *Pulp Fiction* materialized, Jackson, his wife, and his daughter were just about to leave Los Angeles and return to New York. A script arrived in a big brown wrapper from Jersey Films. Jackson read it and couldn't believe it. Sam doesn't insist on liking the characters he plays; merely on understanding them. At an audition for the part of Jules, a producer unwittingly offended Sam by saying, "I love your work Mr. Fishburne." Following a "cold" reading, another actor was being considered for the role. At a second session, Samuel L. Jackson closed the deal.

Portraying Jules, a Bible-quoting Jheri-Kurled hit man in *Pulp Fiction*, he shoots at a man and remarks, "Oh, I'm sorry; did I break your concentration?" Jules afforded Sam an onscreen occasion to call on the fury and demons within him. The actor recalls, "The first time I saw *Pulp Fiction* it actually brought me to tears at the end. I was so pleased to be a part of the film." A framed cover of *Entertainment Weekly* with Sam and the cast of *Pulp Fiction* was proudly on display in his office. Sam likes words; a wordsmith and experienced stage actor, Jackson displays his expert mastery of voice in the film's lengthy soliloquies. Three years following *Pulp Fiction*'s release, it was still the standard against which Jackson's work was appraised. A *New York Times* critic reviewing *Jackie Brown* wrote, "Samuel L. Jackson's role is even splashier than the one he had in *Pulp Fiction* and his performance is even more of a treat." Adulation is rarely unanimous. One critic found "the extreme 'Afro' distracting to the point of reducing Jules to a minstrel, not to be taken seriously, a wacko or funky puppet in the white Tarantino plantation, preaching and mouthing gobble de gook he probably doesn't understand." Not so the Actors Branch of the Academy, which not only understood the role but honored Sam with an Oscar nomination.

Interestingly, as a child, whenever the Oscars were telecast, Sam would stand in front of a mirror and pretend to be giving an acceptance speech. Now that the event had become a real possibility, he guarded against overoptimism about winning. If he lost, Sam bet a friend, he would not smile and applaud the winner in the tradition of good sportsmanship, as losers are expected to do. The Oscar went to Martin Landau for his role of Bela Lugosi in *Ed Wood*. Openly disappointed when Landau's name was announced, Jackson's reaction was "Shit!" He did, however, win a British Academy of Film and Television Award for *Pulp Fiction*. Sam knows that he may win an Oscar one of these days, and then he may not, but his satisfaction comes from doing the best work he possibly can. He has been cast several times in roles that were not even written with a black actor in mind.

An African American actor no longer constrained by race, Sam is less interested in characters that are race specific than in just strong characters. A creative craftsman, he can lose himself unrecognizably in a role by using different hairstyles, as anyone who has seen *The Caveman's Valentine* can attest. Responding to criticism that black actors should not take stereotypical roles, Jackson, something of a perfectionist, advises, "You take the job and you find a way to add dignity to that character." He adds, "I never get tired of acting because I have a passion for it. Every time I have an opportunity to do it, I will do it." Sam was one of the busiest actors of the 1990s, making thirty-six films. In 2000, he received a well-deserved star on the Hollywood Walk of Fame and for the first time carried a film alone, the remake of *Shaft*.

Samuel L. Jackson has moved over the years from supporting player, to feature actor, to costar, and finally star. He is considered one of the most celebrated performers today. His extraordinary film close-ups and accompanying conniptions resonate with the unspoken righteous anger of a large segment of the motion picture audience.

1996

Cuba Gooding Jr.

b. January 2, 1968, Bronx, New York

Winner, Best Supporting Actor, 1996
ROD TIDWELL in *Jerry Maguire*

American popular culture embraced a catchy line from the film *Jerry Maguire*: "Show me the money!" Cuba Gooding Jr. foresees that he will be associated with money for the rest of his life. He surely cannot be blamed for tiring of repeating the phrase on cue wherever he goes or for being coerced into uttering it during personal appearances. The expression took on another context for Cuba when he purchased a mansion in Southern California worth millions, because, no doubt, it became the turn of sundry contractors to entreat, "Show me the money!"

Not terribly long ago, Cuba was so poor that he washed cars, delivered groceries, and lived out of his car. His father, Cuba Gooding Sr., was lead singer for the 1970s musical group The Main Ingredient, which recorded the hit "Everybody Plays the Fool." Gooding Jr. made his nonacting performance debut in 1984 before millions of sports fans as part of a break dancing routine at the close of the Los Angeles Olympic Games, a feat he also performed in *Jerry Maguire*. A genuinely religious man, Cuba adheres to Philippians 4:13: "I can do all things through Christ which strengtheneth me." The one thing Cuba will not do in films is to use the Lord's name in vain.

A studio executive once advised director John Singleton that Cuba had too big a nose for stardom. Perhaps remembering Clark Gable's big ears, Singleton cast Cuba in *Boyz 'n the Hood* anyway. This incident could only have marshaled Cuba's resolve to always be prepared to meet opposition. For *Jerry Maguire* he pumped iron prior to being cast to prove that at five feet eleven inches he could handle the physicality of the part. The twenty-eight-year-old actor also shaved his head to play the flamboyant Rod Tidwell. An apocryphal story involves director Cameron Crowe cautioning Cuba that there would be nudity in the film. Cuba, the prankster, responded, "Shut up, fool" and dropped his trousers. This was a far cry from Cuba's recollection of the embarrassment surrounding his first on-screen lovemaking in *Boyz 'n the Hood.* Directed to fondle actress Nia Long's breasts while she was clad only in panties, Cuba described the experience as akin to rape. Hollywood's blasé "take" on such scenes has been, "It's a tough job but someone has to do it." On set, Cuba had every opportunity to be creative. He recalls, "Anything I would come up with, they would say, 'yeah let's try that'!"

In *Jerry Maguire* Gooding portrays Rod Tidwell, a thin-skinned pro football player for the Arizona Cardinals who is as committed to his family as he is to the sport. Showing deep love for his wife and children, Tidwell is emotionally free enough to declare it publicly. Tidwell longs for media attention, the big bucks, first-tier fame, and the respect he feels he has earned. As an articulate and educated man with a degree in marketing, he seeks the kind of contract that will provide financial security for his family when his peak years are behind him. Demonstrating loyalty, he remains the sole client of his agent (Maguire), who is in the throes of a difficult career move. In real life Cuba faced a similar decision, having to leave the relatively small Paradigm Agency in favor of the powerful Creative Artists Agency. In the film, Jerry Maguire tells Rod Tidwell, "You are wildly charismatic!"— a line also appropriate to actor Gooding's own persona.

Jerry Maguire grossed more than $100 million in its first months of release. One critic refers to Cuba's performance as "snap, crackle, pop . . . bouncing off the wall. Everything in him was heightened . . . the walk, the attitude." Another reviewer opined, "The actor actually makes us fall in love with an egomaniac . . . in lesser hands . . . we could have hated this character. What makes Gooding so charismatic is his comfort in his own skin. The actor has such a free range of expression, it's like watching a raw nerve exposed."

A few pundits considered Gooding's nomination as the Academy's "Not Guilty" plea to activist Jesse Jackson's attempted boycott of the previous year's ceremony. Exuberant over his nomination, Cuba mused, "Hi Denzel, damn it feels good brother. Hi Sidney, hopefully

I'll be there some day. I've been so blessed." Responding to the ridiculous query, "Are you going to vote for yourself?" Cuba had two words, "Hell yes!" He declined speculation about his chances of taking home the trophy, but he was quick to tell interviewers that only his death would cause him to miss the spectacular ceremony.

Winning his Oscar, Cuba thanked Tom Cruise, his costar, with an "I love you brother." The two had worked together before in *A Few Good Men*. Gooding's uninhibited acceptance speech and hurried "thank you"s were driven by the rigidly imposed time constraints of the program. The music kicked in too swiftly, forcing Gooding to speak more rapidly, to jump up and down and to exhibit a joyful proclivity for filibustering. "It was one of the greatest honors in my life, " he admits. Gooding placed his Oscar in an illuminated wine cabinet in his dining room. Yet this sanctuary did not shield Cuba's Oscar from harm. He was watching a subsequent year's Oscar ceremony at home when a bit too much revelry with buddies caused the not-so-durable statuette to fall. Happily, the resulting dent has been repaired.

Soon after winning the Oscar, Gooding fell victim to a typical Hollywood syndrome known as "put them down as soon as they are successful." Some of Gooding's post–Academy Award films have been criticized as undermining his Oscar-garnered authority and empowerment as a star. Cuba does not always seek big roles, but he does search for quality roles. Like many Oscar winners before him Cuba erroneously believed he would get all the work he desired and would be able to pick and choose. Although that did not happen, he is at least considered for more non-race-specific roles. This is a notable change, in that it was not so long ago that Cuba was up for roles only to encounter "We're not going black on this film."

If being the source of "comedic shtick" is an indicator of fame, Cuba Gooding Jr. has made it big time. Answering a query, "If you could wave a magic wand and have anything you want, what would it be?" comedian Robert Townsend quipped without missing a beat, "Cuba Gooding's Oscar." In 2002, Gooding got his own star on Hollywood's Walk of Fame. "Pretty awesome" was his reaction.

1996

Marianne Jean-Baptiste

b. April 26, 1967, London, England

Nominee, Best Supporting Actress, 1996
HORTENSE CUMBERBATCH in *Secrets and Lies*

In *Secrets and Lies* Marianne Jean-Baptiste plays a young black op-
tometrist who unexpectedly discovers that her birth mother is a
white woman. Improvisation by the cast rather than a working
script was the order of the day. The actors would improvise and re-
hearse. They got to know their characters, and director Mike Leigh
would provide the circumstances for the characters to interact.
Leigh did not allow Marianne and the other performers to meet if
the characters they played were not connected. His was an organic
approach to the story, with the actors kept unaware of the plot's ultimate resolution. More than fifty years earlier, a similar technique
had been employed in the shooting of *Casablanca*, the 1943 Academy
Award winner for best picture. Leigh calls his process "growing a
movie." He fixes on a story outline, next casts the film, then has the
actors draw out the characters, dialogue, and structure. The film's
first shot of Marianne is at her adopted mother's burial. Without any
words, her facial expression conveys extreme grief worthy of the
finest silent screen emoting. Although Marianne portrayed a pivotal
leading role, three other actors with smaller parts received billing
over her.

One reviewer comments, "Jean-Baptiste radiates a natural good-
ness. And her biggest moments are when she's not speaking. When
she's working up the courage to call her mother, we see desire and
fear. When her mother invites her to a family get-together, we see a

longing to be part of something as well as uncertainty about whether to accept. You can tell from her expression what's at stake." Another critic calls it "a wonderfully restrained uncommonly human performance. Though the actress keeps everything locked down tight, we feel her desire and embarrassment. The balance between her and Brenda Blethyn is like that of a great comedy team: one so hysterical, the other through sadness, grace and patience steadying the whole film." Critic Armond White claims Jean-Baptiste "has the friendliest face in modern movies."

Following completion of the film and prior to her Academy nomination, Marianne could not get work and had to collect unemployment. Then one extremely early morning a telephone call came from her agent inquiring, "How are you feeling?" "How the f—— do you think I'm feeling, you've just woken me up," she retorted. "You've been nominated," he announced. "For what?" was her reply, readily admitting, "I didn't think Oscar," which produced, initially, a "that's nice" response. Once the news registered, Marianne comments, "It's really nice, a nice feeling to know I did some work that is appreciated." Then came the ceremony and Marianne relished, and which actress doesn't, the concept of various famed couturiers offering gowns for the occasion. Pundits believed the Oscar would go to Lauren Bacall for *The Mirror Has Two Faces* as well as for her longevity. When Juliette Binoche was called to the stage, she was not the only one shocked by the upset. For the record, Marianne Jean-Baptiste is the only black British actor to have won an Oscar nomination. She also received a Golden Globe and a BAFTA nomination for her performance in *Secrets and Lies.*

Most people do not know that Marianne is a multitalent: actress, singer, pianist, composer. With Tony Remy, she cowrote the original score for Mike Leigh's *Career Girls.*

Jean-Baptiste was reared in South East London by West Indian parents; her father is half St. Lucian and half French. Given this particular background, not to become embittered by racism may well be the most important challenge Marianne must confront. Just one example of this burden occurred when she was departing from an airport in Brazil with costar Brenda Blethyn after their visit to promote *Secrets and Lies.* Blethyn was passed through without incident while Jean-Baptiste was detained, although their documents were essentially the same. Blethyn had to exit the aircraft and come to her rescue, adding to Marianne's humiliation.

British writers Barry Norman and Stephen Bourne separately suggest that industry racism in both the United States and the United Kingdom will probably relegate Marianne to small roles rather than to parts commensurate with her huge talent. Skin color still dictates cinema casting. Jean-Baptiste declares, "The old (white) men running the industry just have not got a clue. They've got to come to terms with the fact that Britain is no longer a totally white place where people wear long frocks and drink tea. The national dish is no longer fish and chips, it's curry."

Movie fans are already asking, "Whatever happened to . . . ?" Fellow British film actress Kate Winslet received numerous job offers following her Academy Award nomination, while Marianne has been virtually ignored since her nomination. She was not even invited to a celebration organized by British Screen and attended by various new film personalities, including Winslet.

Ironically, in 1998 Jean-Baptiste appeared in the film *A Murder of Crows* with Cuba Gooding Jr., the African American actor who was nominated along with Marianne in 1996. Gooding Jr. took home an Oscar that year.

1997

Spike Lee

b. March 20, 1957, Atlanta, Georgia

Nominee, Best Documentary, 1997
4 Little Girls

4 Little Girls is about the racially motivated bombing of the Sixteenth Street Baptist Church in Birmingham, Alabama, on September 15, 1963. It is a somber incisive inquiry into the deaths of four Birmingham schoolgirls. Unlike much of Mr. Lee's previous work, this impassioned documentary is simple and understated, which gives it a subdued eloquence. Spike's use of jazz themes as musical background contributes to the impact. The film reveals that Birmingham at the time was known as "Bombingham," a place of intense racism. Before the church killings, there had been other bombings in the local area, which some called "Dynamite Hill." Spike not only places the massacre in the context of the civil rights movement but offers touching sketches of the four girls (Denise McNair, Cynthia Wesley, Addie Mae Collins, and Carole Robertson), portraying them as real individuals, not simply as martyrs. Lee intersperses photographs of the girls with footage of their friends, relatives, and others talking about them more than three decades after the crime. The film had extremely limited distribution and deserves a wider and longer run on DVD.

Spike Lee has long been overlooked at Oscar time, and on this occasion he lost to *The Long Way Home*, a depiction of the hardships endured by liberated concentration camp victims following World War II. That Rabbi Epstein's tribute to Holocaust survivors captured the Oscar over Lee's memorial to racial homicide placed, regrettably, Jews and African Americans once again in competition with each other.

Among those who required no reminder of Birmingham's racial violence was Condoleezza Rice, President George W. Bush's national security adviser. A Birmingham native, she remembers vividly the loss of her childhood friends. Lee's film helped to renew interest in the crime. Approximately four decades after the murders, two of the perpetrators (Bobby Frank Cherry and Thomas E. Blanton Jr., both now elderly men) were finally brought to justice for this heinous act. The other two conspirators from what was considered the most violent urban Klan unit in American history are deceased.

1999

Michael Clarke Duncan

b. December 10, 1957, Chicago, Illinois

Nominee, Best Supporting Actor, 1999
JOHN COFFEY in *The Green Mile*

Bruce Willis, with whom he acted in *Armageddon*, told Duncan about *The Green Mile*, saying, "You are this character. . . . I'm going to call Frank Darabont [the director] and the rest is up to you." Once Willis made the recommendation, he advised Duncan, "Don't embarrass me, make me proud." The Chicago-born actor did precisely that. Although Duncan was six feet five inches, 280 pounds, his preparation for the part required that he add fifty more pounds under the guidance of a nutritionist. He would eat every few hours at home and on the set.

Michael Clarke Duncan had come a long way from his early days in Chicago, where he was once homeless, sleeping in a '67 Buick on the lakefront. Later he dug ditches for the People's Energy Gas Company. In February 1990, while still in Chicago, he guested as a blue-collar worker on a segment of the *Oprah* television program. Finally migrating to California, he worked for a time as a bodyguard for performers Martin Lawrence, Michael Jordan, and Will Smith. Prior to making it in films, he was even contemplating filing an application with the Los Angeles Police Department.

Duncan admits, "I'm an emotional person," and he proudly shares a close relationship with his mother. Always protective of him, she would not even approve his playing college football. However, Michael's interest in martial arts training abides. A genuinely moral and spiritual man, Duncan attends the same church as Denzel

Washington, a fellow Oscar nominee in 1999. Guesting on the *Ainsley Harriott* television show, Michael politely refused a champagne toast to his career success in favor of water, declaring, "I never had a drink in my life." Boasting a lively sense of humor, Duncan laughs about being mistaken for Ving Rhames, another talented African American actor, and he jokes about a *Green Mile* poster sent to him, "I wasn't on the poster anymore; you 'whited' me out and that takes a lot of paint."

The Green Mile is based on Stephen King's 1996 novel. Duncan plays John Coffey, a physically huge black man possessed of childlike behavior who is falsely accused and imprisoned for viciously killing two little white girls. Much of his dialogue and demeanor is reminiscent of the character Lennie in of *Mice and Men*. Coffey asks his jailer, "Do you leave the light on after bedtime? I gets a little scared in the dark sometime, if it's a strange place." After viewing a scene of Fred Astaire and Ginger Rogers dancing, Coffey comments, "Why dey's angels like up in heaven!" Coffey's utterance of "Tell the truth boss, I don't know much of anything, never has" raises the inevitable issue of stereotyping. The strength of Duncan's performance cannot negate all the stereotypes. The character possesses inexplicable mystical healing powers and an innate innocence; some see this as symbolic and see a reference to Jesus Christ in John Coffey's initials. Coffey's healing acts border on the sexual—he kisses the wife of the prison warden on the lips to cure her cancer, and he grabs the crotch of a prison guard to heal his urinary infection. During filming of the latter scene, a momentarily mischievous Tom Hanks stuffed his crotch with a long plastic water bottle, causing Duncan to wonder what he was actually feeling.

Duncan shed real tears in the film and imbued the part with authenticity. During a scene when a posse of whites closes in on his character, their rifles drawn, Duncan confides, "Although I knew it was acting, it was real, they scared me every single take." One writer refers to Coffey as "simpleton savior" and another accuses the Academy voters of having a predilection for subjugated African American characterizations.

On hearing about his Academy nomination, Duncan wept, hollered, and screamed, "I am in there . . . now I can . . . be Academy Award nominee Michael Clarke Duncan. It's kind of cool." Arriving late for the traditional nominees' pre-Oscar luncheon because he lost his house keys and didn't have anywhere to sleep the night before, he prompted then Academy President Robert Rehme to comment, "This may be the first year a homeless person has been nominated." Eschewing false humility, Duncan admitted, "I would love to win an Oscar," and with his usual jocularity added, "It doesn't matter who wins because I'm going to take it from them."

Displaying his strong family orientation, Duncan invited his mother, sister, and niece to the ceremony. Suiting up with a tuxedo is no easy feat for the generously proportioned actor. The Beverly Hills Rochester Big and Tall Store had to accommodate a size 19 ½ neck and a size 54–55 frame. Duncan is the tallest Oscar nominee on record. At the ceremony, emcee Billy Crystal, spoofing the often-quoted line from *The Sixth Sense*, "I see dead people," joked that Duncan was quite likely thinking secretly, "I see white people." Crystal was alluding to the virtually all-Caucasian Oscar audience. Duncan referred to the entire experience as "like being at a premiere times one hundred or like being in a Toys 'R Us store."

Accepting his loss to Michael Caine for *The Cider House Rules* with characteristic graciousness, Duncan pronounced with humor and optimism, "There are not a lot of roles for big, black bald-headed men but hopefully *The Green Mile* will change that." Who knows better than Michael Clarke Duncan that dreams do come true?

1999

Denzel Washington

b. December 28, 1954, Mount Vernon, New York

Nominee, Best Actor, 1999
RUBIN CARTER in *The Hurricane*

Compatible with the film's title, Denzel Washington acts up a storm in *The Hurricane*. The role let Denzel blend the "sweet science" of boxing with the "sweet art" of acting. He turns in a volatile and mesmerizing performance. Family and children have long been in the forefront of this spiritual man's life. Denzel's long-standing commitment to working with youngsters, particularly the Boys and Girls Clubs of America, was acknowledged in 1997 by the Los Angeles Urban League. The organization presented him with its highest honor, the Whitney M. Young Award. Acting has always been in the cards, as it were. In his mother's beauty salon when he was a twenty-year-old college dropout, a prophetic incident occurred. A woman wrote on a sheet of paper, "This boy is going to speak to millions of people." As unlikely as it seemed at the time, Denzel saved the paper with the words that later became very much a reality. Despite the ardor of his countless fans, Denzel sees himself not as a movie star but as a craftsman, an actor. "I've been allowed to use my God-given talent to express these men's opinions," Denzel says, referring to his film portrayals of Malcolm X, Steven Biko, and Rubin Carter.

Having read Carter's touching autobiography, Denzel expressed to producers his abiding interest in the role whenever it was set to go. The actor had never read anything quite like this inspirational story of hope, survival, and endurance. Forming a friendship with

Carter years before making the film, Denzel came to love him like a brother. The actor is noted for his meticulous research in preparing for a role, and *The Hurricane* was no exception. He worked out, trained, and boxed daily. Using no stand-in for the boxing sequences, he took a lot of punishment in the rib area. Running six miles every other day, losing forty pounds, and agreeing to appear nude for the solitary confinement scene are just some of the sacrifices Denzel made in the interest of bringing reality to the role. The film's director, Norman Jewison, and Washington were acquainted, having worked together on *A Soldier's Story* in 1984.

The Hurricane's plot centers on the life of Rubin Carter, a promising middleweight contender who was wrongfully convicted of a brutal triple murder in a Patterson, New Jersey, tavern in 1966. Exonerated after spending two decades imprisoned, Carter was released in 1985. We see the dichotomy of a character who is on one hand positive, self-disciplined, and focused, and on the other hand negative, self-destructive, and volatile. Carter is willing to endure unspeakable punishment rather than wear prison garb. We see a man so disillusioned that he resists love and abandons hope. Poignant are the scenes between Carter (Washington) and Lesra (Vivellous Shannon), the boy who champions his cause. Their scenes together allow Denzel to show nuances of tenderness and emotional vulnerability as a counter to the many moments of explosive rage and ferocity. Denzel's knockout performance (pun intended) amounts to a veritable gamut that includes boxing in the ring, struggling for a shred of dignity as defiant prisoner, and becoming emotionally available to those who try to help him. Carter declares, "Hate put me in prison, love got me out," which is essentially the film's theme. Carter's line "I committed no crime, a crime has been committed against me" is reminiscent of the dramatic use of literary antithesis in *Malcolm X* when Washington proclaims, "We didn't land on Plymouth Rock, Plymouth Rock landed on us."

Those critical of the film claimed that Carter becomes an unblemished martyr rather than a flawed human who was treated unjustly by a racist criminal justice system and that Carter's oppressors are overstated, representing unmitigated evil. Denzel's performance engendered unanimous praise despite the picture's mixed notices. Rubin Carter himself jested, "Until I saw Denzel up on the screen, I didn't know how good looking I was." Critic Rex Reed observed, "Denzel Washington gives the most dynamic performance of his career." Even

President Bill Clinton, guesting on Roger Ebert's television show, singled out Denzel's performance as "Oscar worthy."

On hearing of his fourth nomination for an Academy Award, Denzel acknowledged that being recognized by one's peers is great—but unlike those who claim that it's great just to be nominated, he concedes that he wanted to win. Sidney Poitier viewed Denzel's potential Oscar win from a very personal perspective, arguing that he had waited far too long as the only African American to win an Oscar as best actor in a leading role. Denzel takes the position that once you have done your best work there is little you can do to improve your chances of winning. There is more than a tinge of irony in the fact that the two African American actors nominated in 1999, one in a leading role (Washington) and one in a supporting role (Michael Clarke Duncan) both played characters who are incarcerated. Although Oscar passed Denzel by in favor of Kevin Spacey for *American Beauty*, he did win a Golden Globe Award; his acceptance speech was a succinct "God is love." Admitting the comparable quality of the Spacey and Washington performances, African Americans believed that Washington should have won, because as a Caucasian Spacey will have more opportunities than Washington over the years to demonstrate his Oscar caliber.

Motion picture fame exacts a price. Not too long ago, running briefly in a New York club was a show with the bizarre title "See You in Hell, Denzel: A Psycho-Comedy."

Washington's film characterizations of a military officer, attorney, musician, clergyman, detective, journalist, and so on have paved the way for upcoming African American actors like Wesley Snipes, Andre Braugher, Blair Underwood, and others to be liberated from "uplift the race" roles. As Sidney Poitier had done for him, so Denzel Washington now passes the torch along.

2001

Halle Berry

b. August 14, 1968, Cleveland, Ohio

Winner, Best Actress, 2001
LETICIA MUSGROVE in *Monster's Ball*

Halle Berry has every reason to be pleased with the progression of her career. Named after the Halle Brothers department store in Cleveland, she moved from successive early triumphs such as Miss Teen Ohio, Miss Teen All America in 1985, and runner-up to Miss U.S.A. She also takes pride in her service as a spokesperson for the Juvenile Diabetes Association.

Prior to her work in *Monster's Ball*, Halle's greatest achievement was the HBO film *Introducing Dorothy Dandridge*, for which she earned Golden Globe, Screen Actors Guild, and Emmy awards as best actress. Berry bears a striking resemblance to Dandridge, who was the first African American actress to be nominated for an Academy Award in a leading role. Discovering early on that such luminaries as Whitney Houston and Janet Jackson were considering Dandridge projects of their own became a test of Halle Berry's personal determination to stay the course. She feels a special bond with Dandridge, who was born in the same Cleveland hospital and who was close to Ms. Berry's age when she received her Oscar nomination in 1954.

Berry admits to being eager to play Leticia in *Monster's Ball*, a part that comes along all too infrequently, one that Academy Award nominee Angela Bassett had turned down as demeaning. Berry claims to have read the script in forty-five minutes, which rarely happens. She auditioned more than once and agreed to a salary of

$100,000, a comparatively meager sum for the star of a major film. At first, director Marc Forster and producer Lee Daniels believed Berry to be unsuitable because of her uncontested extraordinary beauty. Early in her career, Halle had to persuade director Spike Lee to cast her as a homeless crack addict in his *Jungle Fever*, a role that Halle was determined to play. This time around Berry knew that as a sensitive young black woman she understood Leticia. She managed finally to convince Forster that despite her gorgeous exterior, she was no stranger to inner turmoil, struggle, heartbreak, frustration, and pain. Leticia's character is the centerpiece of *Monster's Ball*, leaving one to wonder why Berry received on-screen billing after actor Heath Ledger, a relative newcomer in a small role. That Ledger was managed by Daniels, the film's producer, could be a reason. Leticia Musgrove is the wife and then widow of a convicted murderer whose execution is conducted by a racist death-row guard. Subsequently Leticia enters into a mutually desperate sexual relationship with that guard, neither party being aware of their tragic connection. As a waitress and single mother of a twelve-year-old boy, Leticia struggles to eke out a living, to avoid imminent eviction, and to deter her overweight son from his out-of-control addiction to candy bars. For authenticity, the film was shot on location at the Louisiana State Penitentiary at Angola and completed in three weeks. Wearing no makeup, forcing herself as a nonsmoker in real life to chain-smoke (herbal cigarettes were used for this purpose), and stripping to the buff for a required raw sex scene, Berry transformed herself fully into the character. One moment she is cuddling her son, the next she is lashing out at him; one moment she is quietly reflecting in the absence of any dialogue, the next she is evoking a loud emotional outburst. The performance has brought her praise and a reputation as an actress of impressive range. *Rolling Stone* called Halle's performance unforgettable. The *New York Times* wrote, "Ms. Berry proves herself to be an actress of courage and insight. . . . [I]t is above all Ms. Berry's fearless concentration that converts potential sentimentality into honest complex emotion."

A precursor of her Oscar victory was her recognition by the National Board of Reviewers, the Screen Actors Guild, the Golden Globes, the Berlin Silver Bear, and others, in the form of a nomination and/or a win. Film critic Roger Ebert predicted, "Halle Berry is the clearly the actress of the year! She deserves the Oscar." Someone advised Halle's husband, composer-singer Eric Benet, whose songs she inspires, that he should bring some smelling salts to the Oscar ceremony in case she wins. Knowing herself, Berry admitted that it took time to wrap her brain around the reality of the moment and that winning would be like having an out-of-body experience. How right she was became evident when Russell Crowe announced her name. When she could finally utter words, her acceptance remarks revealed her genuine sense of humility: "this moment is so much bigger than me. This moment is for Dorothy Dandridge, Lena Horne, Diahann Carroll. It's for the women who stand beside me, Jada Pinkett, Angela Bassett, Viveca Fox, and it's for every nameless faceless woman of color that now has a chance because this door tonight has been opened." Whether the door has actually been opened remains a hot topic for debate. Oscar nominee Samuel L. Jackson realistically sees it for what it is, Academy recognition of one talented and very attractive African American actress, nothing more.

Just seven years ago, Halle Berry was turned down for a role as a park ranger in the film *Broken Arrow* because some executive thought there were no black park rangers. Because of *Monster's Ball*, Halle Berry's career is indelibly different. She now commands between $6 and $7 million per film. Immediately following her Oscar triumph she went on location as the sexy Jinx in the latest James "007" Bond thriller *Die Another Day*, a sublime example of nontraditional casting.

2001

Will Smith

b. September 25, 1968, Philadelphia, Pennsylvania

Nominee, Best Actor, 2001
MUHAMMAD ALI in *Ali*

The statement "where there's a will, there's a way" assumes special meaning when it pertains to Will Smith. In a meteoric career as a rapper, star of the hit television series *The Fresh Prince*, and then popular hero of a few blockbuster action and sci-fi movies, Smith went on to portray Muhammad Ali and garner an Academy Award nomination as best actor for his performance. Such an honor certainly supports those of the opinion that rappers are natural actors. His role as a con artist in the 1993 film *Six Degrees of Separation* was a prognosticator that Will Smith is a serious actor and immune to stereotypical categorization. Oddly, although he has been eligible for years, Smith only just recently became a member of the Screen Actors Guild.

The actor had some ambivalence about accepting the awesome responsibility of playing the most recognized man on the planet, a bona fide legend in his own time. Will didn't want to be the guy who sullied that image. Yet the actor truly believed that the role was one he was born to play. He was excited but simultaneously petrified at the challenge. Michael Mann, a meticulous director, put Smith through his paces in a tough regimen of preparation: physical, mental, and spiritual. Will trained for a year before the shoot, gaining approximately thirty pounds by eating like a maniac. He was also required to have his ears taped to his head to more closely resemble Ali. Smith undertook dialect training, learning to master the distinctive cadence of the champ's delivery. He engaged in Islamic study in addition to consulting a former Black Panther leader to better understand the volatile era of Vietnam and Civil Rights as it related to Ali's life. Smith had to simulate Ali's boxing moves in order to be credible in the fighting scenes. In spite of "nailing" Ali's fancy footwork, Smith absorbed some serious blows. As a genuine rapport emerged between the two kindred spirits, the actor couldn't resist teasing the champ whenever Ali visited the set with comments like "I'm faster than you were and I'm prettier than you were." It is known that Will Smith put up part of his own salary to cover possible cost overruns. That Hollywood even made a major feature film about such a controversial African American represents progress of a kind.

Will Smith's nomination provided an unprecedented new chapter to the evolving saga of African Americans and their quest for the elusive Oscar. Only once before, in 1972, had three blacks (two actresses, one actor) been nominated for leading role performances, but never before had two black actors been nominated in this category in the same year. Academy members seem to have a predilection for nominating actors in pugilist roles—DeNiro in *Raging Bull*, Stallone in *Rocky*, and Newman in *Somebody Up There Likes Me*. Naysayers predicted the film's disappointing box office and mixed critical reviews would jeopardize a nomination for Smith, but they were wrong.

Although Will Smith went on record as wanting Denzel Washington to win and publicly accepted a "low man on the totem pole" stance with regard to his own possible win, he was open in his joy over being a part of the Oscar nominee group. Smith recognized that from here on he would become Mr. Will Smith, Oscar nominee, even without wearing, as he did, an Ozwald Boateng tuxedo and strolling down the red carpet. Months after his Oscar loss, Will Smith received a BET award as best actor of the year for his film portrayal of Muhammad Ali. At the same ceremony, Ali was honored with BET's Humanitarian Award.

Three leading-role nominations of African American actors means just that, three nominations and nothing more. In a moment of humility rarely seen in Hollywood, Will Smith conceded that there have been black actors before him who may have been even more deserving who didn't get nominated. It would be the height of naïveté to suggest that the barrier of traditional race-based casting has been lifted. Novelist John Grisham's reported dissatisfaction with the possible casting of Will Smith in the film version of his *The Runaway Jury* is a case in point. A level playing field is yet to come.

2001

Denzel Washington

b. December 24, 1954, Mount Vernon, New York

Winner, Best Actor, 2001
ALONZO HARRIS in *Training Day*

Not a very long time following his parents' divorce, Denzel Washington's thoughts turned to a career in acting. First at Fordham University he successfully appeared as Othello and Emperor Jones, and later he studied at the American Conservatory Theater in San Francisco.

The character Alonzo Harris in *Training Day* has been described variously as adrenaline-charged, abrasively streetwise, hot-wired, and as a seductive sociopath. Deciding to accept the part of a narcotics cop gone wrong, a role markedly different from the heroic figures he usually plays, posed no fear for the actor. For what it was worth, even his adolescent son wanted him to do it. Arguably one of the great actors of his time, Denzel as Alonzo was transported to a place outside anything he had done previously. The script unfolds over a twelve-hour period, allowing the character to exude menace shifting from sardonic humor to malevolent aggression. Committing a theft of drug money as well as murder, Alonzo has no redeeming qualities. He becomes the criminal he had been charged to root out. While approaching the character from the inside out, Denzel was not above using such external accouterments as silver chains, black leather jacket, and skullcap to nail the part.

Oscar nominations are considered by some to be a spectator sport. Once nominees are announced, the informal betting and speculation begins, those pro and con line up. Militating against an Oscar win for Washington was a weak script, the release of his poorly received film *John Q*, and losing SAG and Golden Globe Awards to Russell Crowe in *A Beautiful Mind*. Favoring a win for Denzel was his victory at the American Film Institute's first award ceremony. Although he was playing a moral monster, a villainous role can be rewarded with an Oscar, as was Anthony Hopkins's Hannibal Lecter in *The Silence of the Lambs*.

Julia Roberts, who won the best actress Oscar in 2000, had gone on record as claiming that she could not conceive of having a best acting Oscar when Denzel, her costar in *Pelican Brief*, whom she deemed the best actor of his generation, had yet to receive one. As Roberts opened the envelope and saw that Denzel was the winner, she gushed, "I love my life," adding a touching personal moment to Denzel's victory. Washington would have been well within his rights had he quoted one of Alonzo's lines from *Training Day*, "King Kong ain't got nothing on me." Oscar history is rife with nominees who did not win for their best performances but for lesser ones in a subsequent year, perhaps as a consolation prize. Many opine that Washington should have won in 1999 for *The Hurricane*. In his customary dignified manner, Denzel took the statuette from Julia and proclaimed, "God is good, God is great." In gracious acknowledgement of Sidney Poitier, who had earlier in the ceremony acquired an honorary Oscar, Washington spoke, "Forty years I've been chasing Sidney. They finally give it to me and what do they do? They give it to him the same night. I'll always be chasing you Sidney. I'll always be following in your footsteps. There's nothing I would rather do, sir. Nothing I would rather do. God bless you."

Denzel Washington now holds the record as the only African American actor to have won two Oscars in annual competition. He currently commands $20 million per film, joining the ranks of the pricier megastars. In 2002, he completed his first film as a director, a career path on which he intends to continue. In *Training Day*, the corrupt Alonzo Harris utters a line, "Play the game, grow wise and then you can change things," perhaps an apt metaphor for Denzel Washington's personal journey as an African American in the film industry.

2002

Queen Latifah

b. March 18, 1970, East Orange, New Jersey

Nominee, Best Supporting Actress, 2002
MAMA MORTON in *Chicago*

To those who considered the Academy Award nomination of former rapper Will Smith to have been an anomaly, the nomination of Queen Latifah for her role in the widely acclaimed musical *Chicago* put that notion to rest forever. The latter-day rapper, born Dana Owens, played a corrupt prison matron in a strong but brief on-screen appearance. Casting for the role was highly competitive, with names such as Bette Midler, Kathy Bates, and Rosie O'Donnell being mentioned, but after three successful auditions, Latifah got the part. With her customary humour she banters that given a character as complex as Mama, the producers had to throw in some complexion. Provocatively dressed as a flapper, Latifah sings a dynamite double entendre showstopper, "When You're Good to Mama." Another showy number, "Class," was not seen but will possibly be included in the DVD release. All the collective hype for the movie had to con-tribute to Latifah's nomination—or, as her character declares in the film, "You couldn't buy that kind of publicity." Winning Oscar or not, the nomination has elevated Latifah to new status. She correctly views just the nomination as a victory.

Filmography

Margaret Avery

Blueberry Hill 1988
The Color Purple 1985
Cool Breeze 1972
The Fish That Saved Pittsburgh 1979
For Us, the Living 1983
Heat Wave 1990
Hell Up in Harlem 1973
The Lathe of Heaven 1980
Magnum Force 1973
Mardi Gras for the Devil 1993
The Return of Superfly 1990
Riverbend 1990
The Sky Is Gray 1980
Which Way Is Up? 1977

James Baskett

Comes Midnight 1940
Gone Harlem 1939
Harlem Is Heaven 1932
The Policy Man 1938
Song of the South 1946
Straight to Heaven 1939

Angela Bassett

Boesman and Lena 2000
Boyz 'n the Hood 1991
City of Hope 1991
Contact 1997
Critters 4 1992
F/X 1986
The Heroes of Desert Storm 1992
How Stella Got Her Groove Back 1998
Innocent Blood 1992
The Jacksons: An American Dream 1992
Kindergarten Cop 1990
Malcolm X 1992
Music of the Heart 1999
Panther 1995 (cameo)
Passion Fish 1992
The Score 2001
Strange Days 1995
Sunshine State 2002
Supernova 2000
Vampire in Brooklyn 1995
Waiting to Exhale 1995
What's Love Got to Do with It? 1993

Halle Berry

B*A*P*S 1997
Boomerang 1992
Bulworth 1998
Die Another Day 2002
Executive Decision 1996
Father Hood 1993
The Flintstones 1994
Girl 6 1996
Introducing Dorothy Dandridge 1999
Jungle Fever 1991
The Last Boy Scout 1991
Losing Isaiah 1995
Monster's Ball 2001
The Program 1993
Queen 1993
Race the Sun 1996

The Rich Man's Wife 1996
Ringside 1999
Solomon and Sheba 1995
Strictly Business 1991
Sword Fish 2001
Victims of Fashion 1999
The Wedding 1998
Why Do Fools Fall in Love? 1998
X Men 2001

Adolph Caesar

Bird on a Wire 1990
Breakin' 2: Electric Boogaloo 1984
Che! 1969
City Heat 1984
Club Paradise 1986
The Color Purple 1985
Eddie and the Cruisers 1983
The End 1978
The Escape Artist 1982
Fortune Dane 1986
Ghettoblaster 1989
The Hitter 1978
Hot to Trot 1988
I Remember Harlem 1981 (narrator)
Men of Bronze 1977 (narrator)
The Offspring 1987
Retribution 1988
Roadside Prophets 1992
A Small Circle of Friends 1980
A Soldier's Story 1984

Diahann Carroll

Carmen Jones 1954
Claudine 1974
The Five Heartbeats 1991
From the Dead of Night 1989
Goodbye Again 1961
Hurry Sundown 1967
I Know Why the Caged Bird Sings 1978

Paris Blues 1961
Porgy and Bess 1959
Sister, Sister 1982
The Split 1968

Rupert Crosse

The Reivers 1969
Shadows 1961
To Trap a Spy 1966
Too Late Blues 1962
Waterhole # 3 1967

Dorothy Dandridge

Atlantic City 1944
Bahama Passage 1942
Bright Road 1953
Carmen Jones 1954
A Day at the Races 1937
The Decks Ran Red 1958
Drums of the Congo 1942
Ebony Parade 1947
Flamingo 1947
Four Shall Die 1940
The Harlem Globetrotters 1951
Hit Parade of 1943 1943
Island in the Sun 1957
Jungle Queen 1951
Lady from Louisiana 1941
Lucky Jordan 1942
Malaga 1962
Moo Cow Boogie 1943
Murder Men 1960
Pillow to Post 1946
Porgy and Bess 1959
Remains to Be Seen 1953
Since You Went Away 1944
Sun Valley Serenade 1941
Sundown 1941
Tamango 1959
Tarzan's Peril 1951

Jaye Davidson

Catwalk 1995 (documentary)
The Crying Game 1992
Stargate 1994

Michael Clarke Duncan

Armageddon 1998
Breakfast of Champions 1999
Bullworth 1998
The Green Mile 1999
A Night at the Roxbury 1998
The Planet of the Apes 2001
The Scorpion King 2001
See Spot Run 2000
The Underground Comedy Movie 1999
The Whole Nine Yards 2000

Laurence Fishburne

Apocalypse Now 1979
Bad Company 1995
A Band of the Hand 1986
Boyz 'n the Hood 1991
Cadence 1990
Cherry 2000 1988
Class Action 1991
The Color Purple 1985
Cornbread, Earl and Me 1975
The Cotton Club 1984
Death Wish II 1982
Decoration Day 1992
Deep Cover 1992
Event Horizon 1997
Fast Break 1979
Fled 1996
For Us, the Living 1983
Gardens of Stone 1987
Hearts of Darkness: A Filmmakers Apocalypse 1991
Higher Learning 1994
Hoodlum 1997
Just Cause 1995

King of New York 1990
The Matrix 1999
Miss Evers Boys 1997
A Nightmare on Elm Street 3: Dream Warriors 1987
Once in the Life 2000
Osmosis Jones 2001
Othello 1995
Quicksilver 1986
Red Heat 1988
Rumble Fish 1983
School Daze 1988
Searching for Bobby Fischer 1993
The Tool Shed 1994
Tuskegee Airmen 1995
What's Love Got to Do with It? 1993
Willie and Phil 1980

Morgan Freeman

Along Came a Spider 2001
Amistad 1997
The Atlanta Child Murders 1985
Attica 1980
The Bonfire of the Vanities 1990
Bopha! 1993 (director)
Brubaker 1980
Chain Reaction 1996
Clean and Sober 1989
Clinton and Nadine a.k.a. Blood Money 1988
Death of a Prophet 1981
Deep Impact 1998
Driving Miss Daisy 1989
The Earth Day Special 1990
The Execution of Raymond Graham 1985
Eyewitness 1981
Fight for Life 1987
Glory 1989
Hard Rain 1998
Harry and Son 1980
High Crimes 2002
Hollow Image 1979
Johnny Handsome 1989
Kiss the Girls 1997

Lean on Me 1989
The Long Way Home 1997 (narrator)
Marie 1985
The Marva Collins Story 1981
Moll Flanders 1996
Nurse Betty 2000
Outbreak 1995
The Power of One 1992
Resting Place 1986
Robin Hood: Prince of Thieves 1991
Roll of Thunder, Hear My Cry 1986
Seven 1995
The Shawshank Redemption 1994
Street Smart 1987
The Sum of All Fears 2002
Teachers 1984
That Was Then . . . This Is Now 1985
Under Suspicion 2000
Unforgiven 1992
Welcome to Success 1995
Who Says I Can't Read a Rainbow? 1971

Whoopi Goldberg

The Associate 1996
Bogus 1996
Bordello of Blood 1996
Boys on the Side 1995
Burglar 1987
Clara's Heart 1988
The Color Purple 1985
Comic Relief 1990
Corrina, Corrina 1994
The Deep End of the Ocean 1999
Eddie 1996
Fatal Beauty 1987
Ghost 1990
Ghosts of Mississippi 1996
Girl Interrupted 1999
Homer and Eddie 1990
House Party 2: The Pajama Jam 1991
How Stella Got Her Groove Back 1998
Jumpin' Jack Flash 1986

Kingdom Come 2001
Kiss Shot 1992
A Knight in Camelot 1998
The Lion King 1994 (voice)
The Little Rascals 1994
The Long Walk Home 1991
Made in America 1993
The Magic World of Chuck Jones 1992
Moonlight and Valentino 1995
Naked in New York 1994
National Lampoon's Loaded Weapon I 1993
The Pagemaster 1994 (voice)
The Player 1992
Rat Race 2001
Rudolph the Red-Nosed Reindeer: The Movie 1998 (voice)
The Rugrats Movie 1998 (voice)
Sarafina! 1992
Sister Act 1992
Sister Act 2: Back in the Habit 1993
Soapdish 1991
Star Trek: Generations 1994
The Telephone 1998
Theodore Rex 1996
Wisecracks 1992

Cuba Gooding Jr.

As Good As It Gets 1997
Boyz 'n the Hood 1991
Chill Factor 1999
Coming to America 1988
Daybreak 1993
A Few Good Men 1992
Gladiator 1992
Hitz 1992
Instinct 1999
Jerry Maguire 1996
Judgment Night 1993
Lightning Jack 1994
Losing Isaiah 1994
Men of Honor 2000
A Murder of Crows 1998
Outbreak 1995

Pearl Harbor 2001
Rat Race 2001
Sing 1989
Snow Dogs 2002
Tuskegee Airmen 1995
What Dreams May Come 1998

Dexter Gordon

Awakenings 1990
'Round Midnight 1986
Unchained 1955

Louis Gossett Jr.

Aces: Iron Eagle III 1992
Benny's Place 1982
Blue Chips 1994
The Bushbaby 1970
Carolina Skeletons 1991
The Choirboys 1977
Cover-up 1991
The Deep 1977
Diggstown 1992
El Diablo 1990
Enemy Mine 1985
Father and Son: Dangerous Relations 1993
Father Clements' Story 1987
Finders Keepers 1984
Firewalker 1986
A Gathering of Old Men 1987
A Good Man in Africa 1994
Goodbye Miss 4th of July 1993
The Guardian 1984
He Who Walks Alone 1978
Iron Eagle 1986
Iron Eagle II 1988
It Rained All Night the Day I Left 1978
It's Good to Be Alive 1974
Jaws III 1983
J. D.'s Revenge 1976
The Josephine Baker Story 1991
Keeper of the City 1992

The Landlord 1970
The Laughing Policeman 1974
The Lazarus Syndrome 1979
Leo the Last 1970
Monolith 1993
An Officer and a Gentleman 1982
The Principal 1987
The Punisher 1989
A Raisin in the Sun 1961
The River Niger 1978
Sadat 1992
Skin Game 1971
Straight Up 1988
Sudie and Simpson 1990
To Dance with Olivia 1997
Toy Soldiers 1991
Travels with My Aunt 1972
The White Dawn 1974
Zora Is My Name! 1989

Samuel L. Jackson

Against the Wall 1994
Amos and Andrew 1993
Betsy's Wedding 1990
The Caveman's Valentine 2001
Changing Lanes 2002
Coming to America 1988
Dead Man Out 1988
Deep Blue Sea 1999
Def by Temptation 1990
Die Hard with a Vengeance 1994
The Displaced Person 1976
Do the Right Thing 1989
Eddie Murphy Raw 1987
Eve's Bayou 1997
The Exorcist III 1990
Fathers and Sons 1992
Fluke 1995
Formula 51 2002
Fresh 1994
Goodfellas 1990
The Great White Hype 1996

Hail Caesar 1993
Hard Eight 1997
Jackie Brown 1997
Johnny Suede 1992
Juice 1992
Jumpin' at the Boneyard 1992
Jungle Fever 1991
Jurassic Park 1993
Kiss of Death 1994
The Long Kiss Goodnight 1996
Losing Isaiah 1994
Magic Sticks 1987
Menace II Society 1993
The Meteor Man 1993
Mo' Better Blues 1990
Mob Justice 1991
National Lampoon's Loaded Weapon I 1993
The Negotiator 1998
The New Age 1994
187 1997
Out of Sight 1998 (cameo)
Patriot Games 1992
Pulp Fiction 1994
Ragtime 1981
The Red Violin 1999
The Return of Superfly 1990
Rules of Engagement 2000
School Daze 1988
Sea of Love 1989
The Search for One-Eyed Jimmy 1996
Shaft 2000
A Shock to the System 1990
Simple Justice 1993
Sphere 1998
Star Wars: Episode I: The Phantom Menace 1999
Star Wars: Episode II: Attack of the Clones 2002
Strictly Business 1991
Sydney 1997
A Time to Kill 1996
Together for Days 1972
Trees Lounge 1996
True Romance 1993
Unbreakable 2000
Uncle Tom's Cabin 1987

White Sands 1992
XXX 2002
You're Still Not Fooling Anybody 1997

Marianne Jean-Baptiste

Career Girls 1997 (composer)
The Cell 2000
Don't Explain 2001
How to Make the Cruelest Month 1998
London Kills Me 1991
Mr. Jealousy 1997
A Murder of Crows 1998
The Murder of Stephen Lawrence 1999
New Year's Day 2000
No Where to Go a.k.a. Silent Hearts 1998
Secrets and Lies 1996
Spy Game 2001
The 24 Hour Woman 1999
28 Days 2000
Women in Film 2001

James Earl Jones

Allan Quartermain and the Lost City of Gold 1986
The Ambulance 1990
The Atlanta Child Murders 1985
The Bingo Long Traveling All-Stars and Motor Kings 1976
Blood Tide 1982
By Dawn's Early Light 1990
City Limits 1985
Claudine 1974
Clean Slate 1994
Clear and Present Danger 1994
The Comedians 1967
Coming to America 1988
Conan the Barbarian 1981
Convicts 1991
Cry the Beloved Country 1995
Deadly Hero 1975
Dr. Strangelove 1964
The Empire Strikes Back 1980
The End of the Road 1970

Excessive Force 1993
Exorcist II: The Heretic 1977
Field of Dreams 1989
Gardens of Stone 1987
The Great White Hope 1970
The Greatest 1977
The Greatest Thing That Almost Happened 1977
Grim Prairie Tales 1990
Guyana Tragedy: The Jim Jones Story 1983
Heat Wave 1990
The Hunt for Red October 1990
Jefferson in Paris 1995
Jesus of Nazareth 1977
The Last Elephant 1990
Last Flight Out 1990
The Last Remake of Beau Geste 1977
The Lion King 1994 (voice)
Looking for Richard 1996
Malcolm X 1972 (voice)
The Man 1972
Matewan 1987
The Meteor Man 1993
Naked Gun 33 1/3: The Final Insult 1994
Patriot Games 1992
Paul Robeson 1977
Percy and Thunder 1993
A Piece of the Action 1977
Red Tide 1980
Return of the Jedi 1983
The River Niger 1978
The Sandlot 1993
Searchers 1992
Sommersby 1993
Soul Man 1986
The Swashbuckler 1976
Three Fugitives 1989
True Identity 1991

Queen Latifah

The Bone Collector 1999
Bringing Down the House 2003
Brown Sugar 2002

Chicago 2002
The Country Bears 2002 (cameo)
Hoodlum 1997
House Party 2: The Pajama Jam 1991
Juice 1992
Jungle Fever 1991
Living Out Loud 1998
My Life 1993
Set It Off 1996
Sphere 1998
Who's the Man? 1993

Spike Lee

The Answer 1980
Backbeat 1994
Bamboozled 2000
Clockers 1995
Crooklyn 1994
Do the Right Thing 1989
Drop Squad 1994
4 Little Girls 1997
Get on the Bus 1996
Girl 6 1996
He Got Game 1998
A Huey P. Newton Story 2001
Joe's Bed-Stuy Barbershop: We Cut Heads 1983
Jungle Fever 1991
Malcolm X 1992
Mo' Better Blues 1990
The Original Kings of Comedy 2000
Sarah 1981
School Daze 1988
She's Gotta Have It 1986
Summer of Sam 1999
The 25th Hour 2002

Hattie McDaniel

Affectionately Yours 1941
Alice Adams 1935
Another Face 1935
Babbitt 1934

Battle of Broadway 1938
The Big Wheel 1949
Blonde Venus 1932
The Bride Walks Out 1936
Can This Be Dixie? 1936
China Seas 1935
The Crime Nobody Saw 1937
Don't Tell the Wife 1937
Everybody's Baby 1938
Family Honeymoon 1949
The First Baby 1936
The Flame 1947
45 Fathers 1937
Gentle Julia 1936
George Washington Slept Here 1942
Golden West 1932
Gone with the Wind 1939
The Great Lie 1941
Hearts Divided 1936
Hi, Beautiful 1945
High Tension 1936
Hypnotized 1932
I'm No Angel 1933
Imitation of Life 1934
In This Our Life 1942
Janie 1944
Janie Gets Married 1945
Johnny Come Lately 1943
Judge Priest 1934
Libeled Lady 1936
The Little Colonel 1935
Little Men 1934
Lost in the Stratosphere 1934
The Mad Miss Manton 1938
The Male Animal 1942
Margie 1946
Maryland 1940
Merry-Go-Round of 1938 1937
Mickey 1948
Mississippi Moods 1937
Music Is Magic 1935
Never Say Goodbye 1946
Next Time We Love 1936
Nothing Sacred 1937

Operator 13 1934
Over the Goal 1937
Postal Inspector 1936
Racing Lady 1937
Reunion 1936
Saratoga 1937
The Shining Hour 1938
Shopworn Angel 1938
Showboat 1936
Since You Went Away 1944
The Singing Kid 1936
Song of the South 1947
Star for a Night 1936
The Story of Temple Drake 1933
Thank Your Lucky Stars 1943
They Died with Their Boots On 1941
Three Is a Family 1944
The Traveling Saleslady 1935
True Confession 1937
Valiant Is the Word for Carrie 1936
Washington Masquerade 1932
The Wildcatter 1937
Zenobia 1939

Juanita Moore

Abby 1974
Affair in Trinidad 1952
A Band of Angels 1957
A Child Is Waiting 1963
Deliver Us from Evil 1975
Disney's *The Kid* 2000
A Dream for Christmas 1979
Foxstyle 1986
The Girl Can't Help It 1956
The Green-Eyed Blonde 1957
Imitation of Life 1959
Lydia Bailey 1952
The Mack 1973
Papa's Delicate Condition 1963
Paternity 1981
A Raisin in the Sun 1961
Ransom 1956

Rosie 1968
The Singing Nun 1966
Skin Game 1971
Something of Value 1957
Tammy Tell Me True 1961
Thomasine and Bushrod 1974
Two Moon Junction 1988
Uptight 1968
Walk on the Wild Side 1962
Witness to Murder 1954
Women's Prison 1955

Sidney Poitier

All the Young Men 1960
A Band of Angels 1957
The Bedford Incident 1965
The Blackboard Jungle 1955
Brother John 1971
Buck and the Preacher 1972
Children of the Dust 1995
Cry the Beloved Country 1952
The Defiant Ones 1958
Duel at Diablo 1966
Edge of the City 1957
Fast Forward 1985 (director)
For Love of Ivy 1968
Free of Eden 1999
From Whom Cometh My Help 1949 (documentary)
Ghost Dad 1990 (director)
Go, Man, Go! 1954
Goodbye My Lady 1956
The Greatest Story Ever Told 1965
Guess Who's Coming to Dinner? 1967
Hanky Panky 1982 (director)
In the Heat of the Night 1967
The Jackal 1997
Let's Do It Again 1975
Lilies of the Field 1963
Little Nikita 1988
The Long Ships 1964
The Lost Man 1969
Mandela and DeKlerk 1997

The Mark of the Hawk 1958
No Way Out 1950
The Organization 1971
Paris Blues 1961
A Patch of Blue 1965
Paul Robeson: Tribute to an Artist 1979 (narrator)
A Piece of the Action 1977
Porgy and Bess 1959
Pressure Point 1962
A Raisin in the Sun 1961
Ralph Bunche: An American Odyssey 2000 (narrator)
Red Ball Express 1952
Separate but Equal 1991
Shoot to Kill 1988
The Slender Thread 1965
Sneakers 1992
Something of Value 1957
Stir Crazy 1980 (director)
They Call Me Mr. Tibbs 1970
To Sir, with Love 1967
Uptown Saturday Night 1974
Virgin Island 1960
A Warm December 1973
The Wilby Conspiracy 1975

Beah Richards

Beloved 1998
Big Shots 1987
The Biscuit Eater 1972
A Dream for Christmas 1979
Drugstore Cowboy 1989
Gone Are the Days 1963
The Great White Hope 1970
Guess Who's Coming to Dinner? 1967
Homer and Eddie 1990
Hurry Sundown 1967
In the Heat of the Night 1967
Inside Out 1987
Mahogany 1975
The Miracle Worker 1962
Sophisticated Gents 1981

Take a Giant Step 1961
Zora Is My Name! 1989

Howard E. Rollins Jr.

Children of Times Square 1986
Drunks 1996
For Us, the Living 1983
The House of God 1984
On the Block 1991
Ragtime 1981
A Soldier's Story 1984

Diana Ross

Lady Sings the Blues 1972
Mahogany 1975
The Wiz 1978

John Singleton

Baby Boy 2001
Boyz 'n the Hood 1991
Higher Learning 1994
Poetic Justice 1993
Rosewood 1997
Shaft 2000

Will Smith

Ali 2001
Bad Boys 1995
Enemy of the State 1998
The Imagemaker 1986
Independence Day 1996
The Legend of Bagger Vance 2000
Made in America 1993
Men in Black 1997
Men in Black II 2002
Six Degrees of Separation 1993
Where the Day Takes You 1992
Wild Wild West 1999

Cicely Tyson

Acceptable Risks 1986
The Autobiography of Miss Jane Pittman 1974
Benny's Place 1982
The Blue Bird 1976
Bustin' Loose 1981
The Comedians 1967
The Concorde: Airport '79 1979
Duplicates 1992
Fried Green Tomatoes 1991
The Heart Is a Lonely Hunter 1968
Heat Wave 1990
A Hero Ain't Nothin' but a Sandwich 1978
Hoodlum 1997
Just an Old Sweet Song 1976
The Kid Who Loved Christmas 1990
King 1978
The Last Angry Man 1959
Mama Flora's Family 1998
A Man Called Adam 1966
The Marva Collins Story 1981
Odds against Tomorrow 1959
Oldest Living Confederate Widow Tells All 1994
The River Niger 1978
Samaritan: The Mitch Snyder Story 1986
Sounder 1972
Twelve Angry Men 1967
Wilma 1977
A Woman Called Moses 1989
The Women of Brewster Place 1988

Denzel Washington

Antoine Fisher 2002
The Bone Collector 1999
Carbon Copy 1981
Courage under Fire 1996
Crimson Tide 1995
Cry Freedom 1987
Devil in a Blue Dress 1995
Fallen 1998

Flesh and Blood 1979
For Queen and Country 1989
The George McKenna Story 1986
Glory 1989
He Got Game 1998
Heart Condition 1990
The Hurricane 1999
John Q 2001
Malcolm X 1992
The Mighty Quinn 1989
Mississippi Masala 1991
Mo' Better Blues 1990
Much Ado about Nothing 1993
The Pelican Brief 1993
Philadelphia 1993
Power 1986
The Preacher's Wife 1996
Remember the Titans 2000
Reunion: The Saga of an American Family 1986
Ricochet 1991
The Siege 1998
A Soldier's Story 1984
Training Day 2001
Virtuosity 1995

Ethel Waters

Bubbling Over 1934
Cabin in the Sky 1943
Cairo 1942
Carib Gold 1955
Gift of Gab 1934
The Heart Is a Rebel 1956
Hot 'n Bothered 1934
International House 1933
The Member of the Wedding 1952
On with the Show 1929
Pinky 1949
Rufus Jones for President 1933
The Sound and the Fury 1959
Stage Door Canteen 1943
Tales of Manhattan 1942

Paul Winfield

Angel City 1980
Back to Hannibal: The Return of Tom Sawyer and Huckleberry Finn 1990
Big Shots 1987
The Blue and the Gray 1982
Blue City 1986
Brother John 1971
Carbon Copy 1981
Catfish in Black Bean Sauce 2000
Cliff Hanger 1993
Conrack 1974
Damnation Alley 1977
Death before Dishonor 1987
Dennis the Menace 1993
For Us, the Living 1983
Go Tell It on the Mountain 1984
Gordon's War 1973
The Greatest 1977
Green Eyes 1976
Guilty of Innocence: The Lenel Geter Story 1987
A Hero Ain't Nothin' But a Sandwich 1978
High Velocity 1973
Huckleberry Finn 1974
Hustle 1975
It's Good to Be Alive 1974
King 1978
The Lost Man 1969
The Mighty Pawns 1987
Mike's Murder 1984
On the Run 1983
Perils of Pauline 1967
Presumed Innocent 1990
R.P.M. 1970
The Serpent and the Rainbow 1988
Sister, Sister 1982
Sophisticated Gents 1981
Sounder 1972
Star Trek II: The Wrath of Khan 1982
The Terminator 1984
Trouble Man 1972
Twilight's Last Gleaming 1978
White Dog 1981

Who's Minding the Mint? 1967
The Women of Brewster Place 1988

Oprah Winfrey

Beloved 1998
The Color Purple 1985
Listen Up: The Lives of Quincy Jones 1990
Native Son 1986
There Are No Children Here 1993
Throw Momma from the Train 1987
The Women of Brewster Place 1988

Alfre Woodard

The Ambush Murders 1981
Blue Chips 1994
Bopha! 1993
Code of Honor 1990
Crooklyn 1994
Cross Creek 1983
Dinosaur 2000
Down in the Delta 1998
Extremities 1986
Follow Me Home 1997
Freedom Road 1978
Funny Valentines 1999
Go Tell It on the Mountain 1984
Grand Canyon 1991
Gulliver's Travels 1996
The Gun in Betty Lou's Handbag 1992
H.E.A.L.T.H. 1980
Heart and Souls 1993
Holiday Heart 2000
How to Make an American Quilt 1995
K-Pax 2001
The Killing Floor 1984
Love and Basketball 2000
Mandela 1987
The Mary Thomas Story 1987
A Member of the Wedding 1997
Miss Evers Boys 1997

Miss Firecracker 1989
Mumford 1999
Passion Fish 1993
The Piano Lesson 1995
Primal Fear 1996
Remember My Name 1978
Rich in Love 1993
Scrooged 1988
Sophisticated Gents 1981
Star Trek: First Contact 1996
Unnatural Causes 1986
What's Cooking? 2000
Words by Heart 1984

Appendix A

Overlooked Worthy Performances by African American Actors

Although Academy members are instructed to nominate and vote solely on merit, numerous intangibles are inevitably involved. These include a desire to reward an exceptional debut performance, to punish an actor for "politically incorrect" public positions, to compensate an actor for a superior performance overlooked in a previous year, or to convey sympathy for an actor who has overcome tragic circumstances. In short, personal considerations are inescapable. The following is a list of the author's own subjective choices over the years:

1933, Paul Robeson, *The Emperor Jones*
1934, Louise Beavers, *Imitation of Life*
*1949, James Edwards, *Home of the Brave*
*1949, Juano Hernandez, *Intruder in the Dust*
1952, Canada Lee, *Cry the Beloved Country*
1952, Ethel Waters, *The Member of the Wedding*
1961, Claudia McNeil, *A Raisin in the Sun*
1964, Ivan Dixon, *Nothing But a Man*
1967, Sidney Poitier, *In the Heat of the Night*
*1972, Richard Pryor, *Lady Sings the Blues*
*1985, Danny Glover, *The Color Purple*
1988, Forest Whitaker, *Bird*

1989, Morgan Freeman, *Driving Miss Daisy*
*1992, Al Freeman Jr., *Malcolm X*
1993, Denzel Washington, *Philadelphia*
*1995, Don Cheadle, *Devil in a Blue Dress*

---

* Supporting Role

Appendix B

African American Oscar Nominees (Non-Acting/Directing)

1967, Quincy Jones, Song, "The Eyes of Love"
1967, Quincy Jones, Score, *In Cold Blood*
1968, Quincy Jones, Song, "For Love of Ivy"
1969, Hugh A. Robertson, Editing, *Midnight Cowboy*
*1971, Isaac Hayes, Song, "Theme from *Shaft*"
1971, Isaac Hayes, Score, *Shaft*
1972, Lonnie Elder III, Screenplay, *Sounder*
1972, Suzanne de Passe, Screenplay, *Lady Sings the Blues*
1978, Quincy Jones, Score, *The Wiz*
1978, Willie D. Burton, Sound, *The Buddy Holly Story*
1980, Willie D. Burton, Sound, *Altered States*
*1983, Irene Cara, Song, "Flashdance . . . What a Feeling"
1983, Willie D. Burton, Sound, *Wargames*
*1984, Stevie Wonder, Song, "I Just Called to Say I Love You"
1984, Charles Fuller, Screenplay, *A Soldier's Story*
*1984, Prince, Score, *Purple Rain*
1985, Quincy Jones, Song, "Sister (Miss Celie's Blues)"
*1985, Lionel Richie, Song, "Say You, Say Me"
*1986, Herbie Hancock, Score, *'Round Midnight*
*1988, Willie D. Burton, Sound, *Bird*
*1989, Russell Williams II, Sound, *Glory*
*1990, Russell Williams II, Sound, *Dances with Wolves*
1992, Ruth E. Carter, Costume Design, *Malcolm X*

1992, William Miles, Documentary, *Liberators*
1994, Willie D. Burton, Sound, *The Shawshank Redemption*
*1994, Quincy Jones, Jean Hersholt Humanitarian Award
1995, Dianne Houston, Short Film, *A Tuesday Morning Ride*
1997, Ruth E. Carter, Costume Design, *Amistad*

---

*Winner

Appendix C

African American Performers of Nominated Songs at Oscar Ceremonies, A Select List

The first year nominated songs were performed at the Academy Awards ceremony was 1945. Seven years later an African American was a performer, and they are now regular participants.

1952   Billy Daniels, "Because You're Mine"
1955   Harry Belafonte, Millard Thomas, "Unchained Melody"
1956   Dorothy Dandridge, "Julie"
1957   Johnny Mathis, "Wild Is the Wind"
1959   Sammy Davis Jr., "High Hopes"
1960   Sarah Vaughan, "Faraway Part of Town"
1961   Johnny Mathis, "Love Theme from *El Cid*"
1964   Nancy Wilson, "My Kind of Town"
1965   Barbara McNair, "The Shadow of Your Smile"
1966   Dionne Warwick, "Alfie"
1967   Louis Armstrong, "The Bare Necessities"
      Sammy Davis Jr., "Talk to the Animals"
1968   Abbey Lincoln, "For Love of Ivy"
      Aretha Franklin, "Funny Girl"
1969   Lou Rawls, "Jean"
1970   Lola Falana, "Till Love Touches Your Life"
1971   Charley Pride, "All His Children"
      Johnny Mathis, "Life Is What You Make It"
      Isaac Hayes, "Shaft"

1972 Michael Jackson, "Ben"
      Diahann Carroll, "Strange Are the Ways of Love"
1974 Aretha Franklin, "I Feel Love"; "Like This Again";
      "Wherever Love Takes Me"
1975 Diana Ross, "Theme from *Mahogany*"
1976 Ben Vereen, "Gonna Fly Now"
1977 Aretha Franklin, "Nobody Does It Better"
1978 Johnny Mathis, "The Last Time I Felt Like This"
1979 Dionne Warwick, "It Goes Like It Goes"
      Sammy Davis Jr., "Songs That Oscar Forgot, A Medley"
1980 Irene Cara, "Fame"; "Out Here on My Own"
1981 Lionel Richie and Diana Ross, "Endless Love"
1982 Patti Austin and James Ingram, "How Do You Keep the
      Music Playing?"
1983 Irene Cara, "Flashdance"
      Donna Summer, "Papa Can You Hear Me?"
      Jennifer Holliday, "The Way He Makes Me Feel"
1984 Ray Parker Jr., "Ghostbusters"
      Deniece Williams, "Let's Hear It for the Boy"
      Debbie Allen, "Footloose"
      Diana Ross, "I Just Called to Say I Love You"
1985 Lionel Richie, "Say You, Say Me"
1986 Natalie Cole and James Ingram, "Somewhere Out There"
      Melba Moore and Lou Rawls, "Take My Breath Away"
1987 Little Richard, "Shakedown"
1989 James Ingram, "After All"
      Patti Austin, "The Girl Who Used to Be Me"
      Geoffrey Holder, "Kiss the Girl"; "Under the Sea"
1991 Peabo Bryson, "Beauty and the Beast"
      Diana Ross, "Over the Rainbow"
1994 Janet Jackson "Again"
      James Ingram, "The Day I Fall in Love"
1995 Vanessa L. Williams, "Colors of the Wind"
1997 Aaliyah, "Journey to the Past"
1999 Mariah Carey and Whitney Houston, "When You Believe"
2000 Ray Charles, "Under My Skin"; "Secret Love"; "All the Way"
      Isaac Hayes, "Shaft"
      Dionne Warwick, "Alfie"
      Queen Latifah, "The Man Who Got Away"; "The Way We
      Were"
2002 Queen Latifah, "I Move On"

Bibliography

Bogle, Donald. *Dorothy Dandridge, A Biography.* New York: Amistad, 1997.

Brode, Douglas. *Denzel Washington, His Films and Career.* Secaucus, N.J.: Carol, 1997.

Carroll, Diahann. *Diahann, An Autobiography.* Boston: Little Brown, 1986.

Collier, Aldore. "The Oscars in Black and White," *Ebony* (April 2000): 90–95.

Cripps, Thomas. *Making Movies Black: The Hollywood Message Movie from World War II to the Civil Rights Era.* New York: Oxford University Press, 1993.

Harkness, John. *The Academy Awards Handbook, 1998.* New York: Pinnacle, 1998.

Hill, George, and Spencer Moon. *Blacks in Hollywood, Five Favorable Years in Film and Television, 1987–1991.* Los Angeles: Daystar, 1992.

Holden, Anthony. *Behind the Oscar, The Secret History of the Academy Awards.* New York: Simon & Schuster, 1993.

Jackson, Carlton. *Hattie: The Life of Hattie McDaniel.* Lanham, Md.: Madison Books, 1990.

Jones, Arnold Wayne. *The Envelope Please: The Ultimate Academy Awards Trivia Book.* New York: Avon, 1999.

Jones, James Earl, and Penelope Niven. *Voices and Silences.* New York: Scribner's, 1993.

Keyser, Lester J., and André H. Ruszkowski. *The Cinema of Sidney Poitier.* South Brunswick, N.J.: A. S. Barnes, 1980.

Klotman, Phyllis R. *Frame by Frame: A Black Filmography.* Bloomington: Indiana University Press, 1979.

Klotman, Phylis R., and Gloria Gibson. *Frame by Frame II: A Filmography of the African American Image, 1978–1994.* Bloomington: Indiana University Press, 1997.

Lee, Spike, with Lisa Jones. *Do the Right Thing.* New York: Simon & Schuster, 1989.

Levy, Emanuel. *And the Winner Is . . . The History and Politics of the Oscar Awards.* New expanded ed. New York: Continuum, 1991.

Mair, George. *Oprah Winfrey.* New York: Harper Collins, 1994.

Maltin, Leonard. *Leonard Maltin's Movie and Video Guide.* New York: Plume, 2001.

Mapp, Edward. *Directory of Blacks in the Performing Arts.* 2nd ed. Metuchen, N.J.: Scarecrow Press, 1990.

Mills, Earl. *Dorothy Dandridge.* Los Angeles: Holloway House, 1991.

Null, Gary. *Black Hollywood from 1970 to Today.* Secaucus, N.J.: Carol, 1993.

Osborne, Robert A. *Seventy Years of the Oscar: The Official History of the Academy Awards.* New York: Abbeville Press, 1999.

Oscar's Greatest Moments, 1971 to 1991 (video). Academy Foundation, 1992. RCA/Columbia Home Video.

Parish, James Robert. *Today's Black Hollywood.* New York: Pinnacle, 1995.

Patterson, Lindsay. *Black Films and Film-Makers: A Comprehensive Anthology from Stereotype to Superhero.* New York: Dodd, Mead, 1975.

Pickard, Roy. *The Oscar Movies.* 4th ed. New York: Facts on File, 1994.

Poitier, Sidney. *This Life.* New York: Knopf, 1980.

———. *The Measure of a Man: A Spiritual Autobiography.* San Francisco: HarperSanFrancisco, 2000.

Rhines, Jesse Algernon. *Black Film, White Money.* New Brunswick, N.J.: Rutgers University Press, 1996.

Ross, Diana. *Secrets of a Sparrow: Memoirs.* New York: Villard, 1993.

Rovin, Jeff. *Richard Pryor: Black and Blue.* New York: Bantam, 1983.

Sackett, Susan. *Hollywood Sings! An Inside Look at Sixty Years of Academy Award–Nominated Songs.* New York: Billboard, 1995.

Turner, Tina. *I, Tina.* With Kurt Loda. New York: Morrow, 1986.

Waters, Ethel. *To Me It's Wonderful.* New York: Harper & Row, 1972

Wiley, Mason, and Damien Bona. *Inside Oscar: The Unofficial History of the Academy Awards.* 10th ed. New York: Ballantine, 1996.

Index

About the Author

Edward Mapp is the author of *Blacks in American Films: Today and Yesterday* (Scarecrow Press, 1972). He also coauthored *A Separate Cinema, Fifty Years of Black-Cast Posters*. A former columnist for *Movie/TV Marketing*, he has published numerous articles and essays about African Americans in film. Dr. Mapp's vast collection of original black-cast film posters were presented in 1996 to the Academy of Motion Picture Arts and Sciences for its Margaret Herrick Library in Beverly Hills, California. The retired college professor resides in New York City.